DANA WHITE
King of MMA

An unauthorized biography

JUNE WHITE

ISBN: 0983634610
ISBN-13: 9780983634614

"It's not who you are, but what you do that defines you."

Batman, the movie

———

"Character, in the long run, is the decisive factor in the life of an individual."

Theodor Roosevelt

To those who have left our family much too soon
and are missed every day;
Jessica Wills, Jason Mraz and Madelyn Wills.

"When this thing is a sport, all over the entire world, and you can take the UFC to any city in any country, just like soccer, then I did it. I did what I set out to do. That's why I was put on this planet. That's my job, my destiny, whatever the (expletive) you want to call it."

Yahoo Sports, July 8, 2009.

TABLE OF CONTENTS

INTRODUCTION

Very few people can take a company on the brink of bankruptcy and turn it into a multibillion-dollar international business in eight short years. What type of person is able to accomplish this feat while keeping the competition from even coming close to taking any part of the market from them?

First, if you know that the initials MMA stand for mixed martial arts, you also know that the UFC is the Ultimate Fighting Championship, the biggest promoter of mixed martial arts in the world. If you know all of that, then you certainly would recognize the name Dana White, King of MMA and President and part owner of the UFC. Dana White was named Promoter of the Year from 2005 to 2008 and Nevada Sportsman of the year in 2009; and in 2010, he was invited to speak at Oxford University, the same place where President Reagan, Mother Teresa, and the Dali Lama have been invited guest speakers.

There are few if any in the world who can claim the titles of President and King. Although Dana can claim both titles, dictator could be another of those titles. Everywhere Dana goes in the world — and the UFC is seen in more than 170 countries and territories — his fans and the fans of MMA treat him like a rock star.

In an article titled "White Makes Hub-Bub" in the *Boston Herald* (August 9, 2009), "White said, 'I'm serious...it doesn't make a difference to me, (but) it's going to happen. And it's going to happen everywhere else all around the world. There's no stopping it." Also high on White's list is holding an event in Mexico. White said the UFC secured a television deal for over-the-air broadcasts in Mexico and noted that the initial results, for the broadcast of UFC 100, were an estimated 25 million Mexican viewers tuning in." This is what Dana's fans love him for, the fact that he has taken the sport of MMA to where it is today, and for Dana, there is no end in sight for the expansion of the UFC and MMA.

Dana became involved in the sport in 2001. After four years of struggling against enormous odds and losing money, the UFC exploded with the introduction of *The Ultimate Fighter* reality show on Spike television in 2005. Now, even in these tough economic times, Dana has had no problem selling out 44,000 seat arenas, and every year the company's profits continue to climb.

The company is now a multi-billion dollar international business, and Dana has made himself a multimillionaire before the age of forty. On a recent business deal, he personally netted 66 million dollars, a far cry from his income in 1993, a mere $10,000.

Dana is interviewed constantly by MMA magazines, MSNBC, *Nightline, 60 Minutes, Time Magazine, Rolling Stone Magazine, Men's Fitness, Playboy* and so many others, and yet he is elusive about who he really is and how he became the person who has grown the sport of MMA and the UFC into what they are today.

Who is the person who has accomplished all of this? I will tell you who Dana White was, who he is today, and the road that took him to his present place at the top of MMA. I have known him all his life. I am his mom.

DANA AND THE UFC

Dana White became involved in the sport of mixed martial arts in Las Vegas, Nevada back in 2000 when, by chance, he met some MMA fighters and started training with them in a gym he ran in Las Vegas. Soon he was representing a couple of these MMA fighters, Tito Ortiz and Chuck Liddell, as their manager. At the time, Dana was teaching boxing aerobics at gyms in Las Vegas and giving private lessons to many of the Las Vegas elite. Who would have ever guessed that a chance meeting with a few MMA fighters would propel Dana into the world of MMA the way it has. In four short years, he has become a multimillionaire and MMA has become a sport seen around the world, including in Canada, Europe, Australia, the Philippines, China, and Mexico. In fact, the UFC has created a monopoly in the world of MMA. Many have tried to take a portion of that monopoly but all have failed. The UFC has the money, resources, and power to dominate the world of MMA and either buys out the competition or drives them out of the sport. Dana is ruthless in his control and dominance of the sport. Sadly, however, that ruthlessness has also spilled into his personal life and relationships.

Those who meet Dana and write about the sport very often refer to him as a colorful and outspoken head of the UFC, and to be certain, Dana is the person responsible for bringing the sport of MMA to where it is today. Few people would dispute that fact. Dana has taken MMA from a little known and little respected sport

— a sport that Senator John McCain once referred to as human cock fighting and campaigned to put an end to — and turned it into a well-recognized international sport that pulls in record revenues. For example, the fights in Boston this summer pulled in more money than any sporting event ever at the Garden.

In the beginning, every state in the country, with the exception of New Jersey, banned the UFC. Today fight results are reported in the mainstream news, 47 states sanction MMA, millions of viewers watch the fights on pay per view, and Harley Davidson and Anheuser-Busch are sponsors (and Bud-Light is the "official beer of the UFC"). In 2006, the UFC's revenues for pay-per-view events surpassed all other pay-per-view programming with over $222,000,000 in buys. In fact, UFC 66, Chuck Liddell vs. Tito Ortiz, was the first non-boxing card to top one million pay-per-view buys in North America. Even in these tough economic times, even in today's recession, the UFC continues to bring millions of dollars into the ailing economy of Las Vegas and to increase their profits year after year.

Zuffa, LLC is the parent company of the Ultimate Fighting Championship, and Dana is President and ten percent owner. Brothers Frank and Lorenzo Fertitta own the other ninety percent. Dana and Lorenzo were classmates at Bishop Gorman High School, a private Catholic school, in Las Vegas. Frank was a few years ahead of Dana in school. In 2005, Dana and the Fertittas produced and aired *The Ultimate Fighter* (TUF) reality show on Spike television, and Spike has since picked up *UFC Unleashed* and *UFC Fight Night*. The UFC has produced live fights in England, Ireland, Canada, Germany, Australia, and Abu Dhabi, six foreign events in a little over a year, as well as fights every month in cities all over the United States. Dana has been working hard to produce a fight in Madison Square Garden in New York City, and I am sure we will see that happening soon.

Many MMA fighters have graced the covers of magazines such as *Sports Illustrated, Men's Fitness,* and *ESPN the Magazine*. Articles on the sport have appeared in *Rolling Stone, Time, USA Today;* and 60 Minutes, MSNBC, and Nightline have produced segments dedicated to MMA. MMA fighters have been guests on many television shows, and some have recently starred in movies. As noted previously, Dana was named Promoter of the Year each year from 2005 to 2008, and for good reason: no one does a better job at promoting any type of sport than Dana. MMA is his passion, and his true love of the sport makes him the perfect person for his job. In fact, to Dana, promoting MMA is not a job but something he loves to get up every day and do. But who is Dana White?

There are many articles written about Dana, where he came from, and the hard life he had growing up. I have heard him referred to as a Southie tuff, but that is not who Dana is and does not accurately reflect the life he has led. It is hard for me to hear the many myths about Dana, and the way he is portrayed to the public. It is difficult for me to see how, as the popularity of the UFC evolved, the person I once knew changed into someone who is egotistical, self-centered, arrogant, and cruel. I liken Dana's transformation to that of the fictional character, in *Lord of the Rings*, (my precious). Just as the ring of power changed that fictional character, Dana's power and wealth have changed him into someone I do not recognize.

Dana's family and friends were always there to help and support him no matter what the circumstances. As Dana's success grew and the circumstances of life changed for him, he did not do the same for them. Dana went from being a true friend, a good son, and a truly nice person to being a vindictive tyrant who lacks any feelings for how he treats others. It is hard to say if what changed him so utterly was the extreme amount of money he came into so quickly, the influence of those around him, or how suddenly he could make or break so many people. Power can create ugly beasts. In meetings that were not going Dana's way, he has told me, he would stand up at the conference table, (creating a psychological advantage), holler, and swear at individuals he was dealing with. He would tell them, "I'll bury you!" Dana has a very short fuse and it does not take a whole lot to set him off on a totally out-of-control tirade. These days he always gets what he wants, no matter what it takes to get it. His employees will echo that same powerful statement: he will do whatever it takes to get what he wants.

A good deal of Dana's power obviously comes from the extraordinary amount of money he has acquired in the last few years. When you have that much money, everyone wants to be your friend, your pal, your buddy, a member of your entourage. True friends are the ones that were there before the houses, cars, planes, fancy trips, and extravagant parties. True friends are the ones who would share a peanut butter sandwich with you when your refrigerator was empty and so were your pockets.

As early as when the UFC had just begun to turn around and the company was making a profit, I could see changes in Dana that bothered me. I would always tell him, "Keep your feet on the ground. Remember who you are and where you came from. Don't let your head get so big you can't fit through a doorway."

He always responded the same way: "You do not have to ever worry about that."

These negative changes in Dana became more and more noticeable. I kept hoping Dana would recognize that he was becoming a different person, that there seemed to be a correlation between his increasing wealth and his increasing unkindness to those around him. I thought he would take a step back and look at what it was he was doing to friends and family. As his mom, if anyone could or should say something, I felt it would be me. Indeed, most people take advice from their moms as constructive, at least as well intended. In an e-mail, I told my son that I wanted my old Dana back. I felt like aliens had abducted my Dana and replaced him with this other person I really did not know. I assumed he would at least think about what I had said and about what it was, he was doing, but his response was the furthest thing from stepping back and thinking about what I had just told him.

Dana immediately e-mailed me back: "Who the fuck do you think you are, talking to me like that? No one talks to me that way."

Of course, after the initial shock faded, I shot back, "I am your mother, that is who I am, and don't you ever forget that. I am not one of your fighters or employees!" That was exactly my point in my initial email to him, that he was treating people as if they were less than deserving of common courtesy and respect.

His next response was not what I had expected either. It was a good thing for him I was on the east coast and he was in Las Vegas. I was so angered by his replies. My blood pressure had to be at stroke level. We did not speak for an extended period after that. This was the upshot of the changes in my son, and it seems to me partly due to a mythology that grew up around him and that he did nothing to correct. In fact, he seems to have helped spread these tales. It is time to set the record straight about who Dana White was and who he has become.

Article after article spreads a myth of the early life of Dana White, how as a child he endured without his mother or father around, how he had no male figures in his life. In this fictional version of his life, Dana was a child left on his own in the mean streets of South Boston and Las Vegas. This picture of his youth is certainly something that makes for good reading but it is a far cry from the truth. The truth is Dana lived a charmed life growing up in a family full of uncles, aunts, cousins, and grandparents who were always around, who were all very close and spent holidays and vacations together. Dana attended private school in Las Vegas, and from kindergarten until he graduated high school, I always stayed on top of what was going on with his academics. When he was faltering or having trouble in school, I immediately took steps to address the problems. While living in Las Vegas, his grandmother, a retired teacher, would go to his school and sit in on his class to see why he was having problems when his grades were poor.

After Dana was born, we spent a year living in a small, rural town in Connecticut. We spent another year in a small beach community in Florida, and a year and a half living in a bedroom community in Connecticut and then seven years living in a quaint little town in rural western Massachusetts. Even after moving to Las Vegas, Dana spent his summers in upstate Maine. Dana never had a job or worked while he lived at home, and he did very little in the way of chores at home. Even after moving out on his own, he frequently came to me for help and support. So much for the boy-raising-himself-in-the-streets myth, but let us start at the very beginning in more detail.

THE BEGINNING

The King of MMA was born Dana Frederick White, Jr. He was born on a Monday afternoon, on July 28, 1969 at 3:02 pm in Manchester, Connecticut. I was nineteen years old and a high school dropout. His father, Dana Sr., was twenty-one years old and worked in the mailroom at Pratt and Whitney Aircraft. Throughout the pregnancy, I did not work. I had been very sick for the first seven months of the pregnancy and actually lost weight up until the eighth month. I had nausea and vomiting that was so severe I could rarely hold down any food and just the smell of food sent me running to the bathroom retching all the way. At times, the vomiting became so severe I would bring up large amounts of blood and clots and have to go to the emergency room to stop the vomiting. My doctors never considered the possibility that my sickness was because I was pregnant. With the weight loss, constant vomiting, and bleeding the doctors had diagnosed me as having a rare blood disease and I was told that I had possibly a year to live. One of the doctors treating me had included a pregnancy test with other blood work and it came back positive, everyone was shocked and very concerned for both my health and Dana's.

I remember my first appointment with the obstetrician. I was sitting in the waiting room with four other women. The women were talking with one another asking how far along they were and when their due date was. Each of them was between five and seven months pregnant. I glanced over to the part of the waiting room where they had all congregated and gave them a quick once over. My first thought was they were very large, I thought to myself "God, what a bunch of cows. How much bigger can they get." None of the women in the room had included me in their conversation or asked me how far along I was, but that was probably because I had no belly sticking out at all. In fact, my hipbones were sticking out. I was nineteen years old and quite ignorant about being pregnant, which looking back now was a blessing in disguise.

The doctors tried to determine how far along I might be and decided I was probably somewhere in my seventh or eighth month of pregnancy, and I was without any prenatal care to that point. The doctors in the emergency room on one of my many visits had decided to admit me to the hospital and do further tests, but Dana's father said no, I was going home. We did not have health insurance at that time, and we did not have the money to pay hospital and doctor bills.

Dana's father and I had to set up a payment plan with the obstetricians caring for me, even though it would only be for a month or two. When I was discharged from the hospital after Dana was born, we had to go to the billing office on our way out of the hospital and the staff who worked in that department informed us we could not leave the hospital without paying our bill in full because we had no insurance. I thought, we're being held hostage by the billing department. After much back and forth, they had us sign a contract agreeing to pay on a monthly installment plan. It felt like when we went to Wal-Mart and put our Christmas presents on lay-away. I thought, "If we miss a payment, what do they do? Make us return him?" Dana was causing us problems and costing plenty from the very beginning of his life.

Dana was born three weeks after my projected due date, weighed six pounds, nine ounces, and was nineteen inches long. He was thin from my constant vomiting and his skin was peeling from being overdue. He was not a pretty baby when he was born, but skinny and scraggly looking. Dana wasn't one of those babies with the chubby thighs but instead with skinny, little chicken legs. For all the difficulties I had during the pregnancy, however, he was born healthy and without any problems. When he was four years old, he was sick with a stomach bug and I brought him to an emergency room, where they picked up something wrong with his heart. By age nine, the doctors felt the problem had resolved itself.

I stayed in the hospital for five days after Dana was born. One afternoon I asked the nurse who had brought Dana in to me if he slept as well in the nursery as he did when he was with me in my room. He was always sleeping. She gave me a quirky side look as if the look should have answered the question and then informed me he was the baby you could hear screaming all night in the nursery. From his earliest days, he has let the world know when he is unhappy. Not much has changed from those first days in the hospital and especially now that he is rich and powerful. If he could have spoken when he was born, I'm sure the f-bomb would have been part of his little tirades in his bouts of screaming all night in the hospital. When I was finally home, I foolishly thought things would return to normal and everything would be fine. What a rude awakening, (even to this day I sympathize with new parents) there was no sleeping at night for a very long four months. Any parent can relate to that kind of sleep deprivation — it is brutal. Every night he would scream and cry all night. Rocking him and feeding him would not stop the screaming, and I thought I would go mad from sleep deprivation. His father once stated, "I think he knows it's time for us to go to bed and he doesn't want any brothers or sisters." The doctor said he just had his days and nights mixed up and it would eventually correct itself.

Rosemary's Baby came out in 1968. The movie starred Mia Farrow as a young woman who, by the end of the movie, has Satan's child. Dana was born in 1969, shortly after this movie came out. One afternoon, when the nurses brought Dana to me for his feeding, thoughts of this movie came back me. I remembered how Mia Farrow was so sick through her pregnancy in the movie, just like I had been with Dana. This was the first time Dana had opened his eyes while he was with me. When I looked into his eyes, I was taken aback by how black his eyes were. I had never seen anyone with eyes so black. My family ancestry is Irish, and so we all have blue or green eyes. I could not tell where Dana's pupils ended and where the color of the iris should have started. The effect was chilling, and I had the feeling of looking into soulless eyes. The experience was truly upsetting and worried me as to who, or what, he would grow up to be.

Of course, being Irish Catholic, I do believe there is good and evil around us and intertwined in our everyday lives. I believe some people are just born evil and, no matter what their lives are like growing up, nothing will change that. The lack of any warmth or dimension to Dana's eyes was unsettling, but after a while, Dana's eyes lightened and softened, the deep blackness in his eyes changed to a soft warm brown. His hair was so blonde it was almost white, and his temperament was that of one of the sweetest, kindest, happiest little boys you would ever meet. He was my little angel. Everyone loved him, and that would not change for many years. Dana's personality is one that people are drawn to him, wanting to be his friend, and that would follow him well into his adult years.

These days, Dana professes to be an atheist and says he does not believe in God or "any of that bullshit." You would think that someone who has had the good fortune in life that he has would believe there is something more to these fortuitous circumstances than just his own efforts or good luck. Of course, some people make statements like that when their personal actions show total disregard for any principles or morals. I suppose, if you believe there are no consequences for your actions on this earth, you don't need to care what you do here and now — a lack of belief nothing more than a free pass for bad behavior. I was in a conversation with a friend, the subject of Dana being an atheist came up, and although this person is Dana's age, his background is similar to mine. Old school Irish Catholic and he said to me, "June think of it this way if Dana is right and there is nothing beyond our life here then we're no worse off for what we believe, but if we are right then Dana is screwed." I thought about it for a minute and laughed, he was right.

10

A few years ago, Dana had hired someone to write about him and this person called to ask me questions about Dana and what he was like growing up. Somewhere in the conversation, he asked me how I felt about Dana being an atheist. I had no idea at the time that Dana was claiming he did not believe there was a God. I responded, "Dana was raised Catholic. He was an altar boy. He went to Catholic school and was married in the Catholic Church and all his children were baptized in the church." Somewhat confused by the news I asked, "When did Dana make this decision?"

Before the writer could answer, I thought about Dana's behavior these days and told the writer, "Oh, wait. I can understand why he doesn't believe in God anymore. It's because these days he thinks he's God." The writer went back to Dana and told Dana that I had made those comments to him. I am told Dana was furious. I found his reaction quite amusing.

Recently, I was in the hospital and very sick, knocking-on-heaven's-door sick. Dana came to see me, and one of the first things he asks me is whether I actually made that comment to the writer about him thinking he was God. I told him I did and thought it was witty for what the writer had asked. I don't think Dana thought so. He has no sense of humor regarding himself anymore, (I am King, hear me roar). In an article in *Rolling Stone* dated June 12, 2008, Dana was quoted as saying his mom thinks he is a "tyrant who thinks he's God."

Manchester Memorial Hospital
Manchester, Connecticut

This Certifies that ____DANA FREDERICK WHITE, JR.____

was born to ___DANA FREDERICK AND ▓▓▓ WILLS WHITE___

in this Hospital at __3:02__ o'clock _P_ m, on _____MONDAY_____

the __TWENTY-EIGHTH__ day of _____JULY_____ 19_69_

In Witness Whereof the said Hospital has caused this Certificate to be signed by its duly authorized officer and its Official Seal to be hereunto affixed.

Edward McKenney
Administrator

Dan A. Sulmo M.D.
Attending Physician

(Seal: THE MANCHESTER MEMORIAL HOSPITAL · INCORPORATED · MAY 8, 1919 · MANCHESTER, CONN.)

FAMILY

Dana's maternal grandfather, Bertram Wills, was born in Somerville, Massachusetts on July 8, 1896; he died when I was sixteen, and his death changed all our lives greatly. Bert was a big man of six foot, two inches and weighing in at around two hundred and fifty pounds. He had a ruddy complexion and thin gray hair combed off to one side. He wore a hat that men in the 1930s wore, and I always liked that, but Bert was a man to be feared. He was both physically and verbally abusive to my siblings, my mother Madelyn (O'Neil), and me. The abuse to Madelyn occurred mostly when Bert was drinking, but for my siblings and me, anything could set him off at any time. Growing up in our household, you always had to be on guard because you never knew when he would erupt. Bert's marriage to Dana's grandmother was his second marriage, and he was twenty-one years older than Madelyn. Bert had two grown children from his first marriage and six children with Madelyn, all of us just fourteen to sixteen months apart. His grandmother, who was from Ireland and who ran a boarding house in Cambridge for the young men who went to Harvard, had raised Bert. He was fiercely proud that he came from Irish ancestry and many a fight erupted in many a bar when some poor soul would suggest that the surname Wills was not Irish but English. He was a huge boxing fan, and he had been an amateur boxer in the Navy, although I understand his record was not anything to brag about.

Dinner was always at five o'clock on the dot, and you better be seated at the table by five or all hell would break loose. Dinner was always meat and potatoes, except on Friday when all Catholics had fish. Dinner at the Wills household was anything but pleasant, it was always very tense and stressful and nothing to look forward to. Bert would go off in a rage with the slightest provocation, which kind of sounds like someone else I know. Something as small as someone holding his or her fork the wrong way would set him off, which in turn sent him into a rage through the rest of the meal, usually causing him to hit one of my two brothers, Dennis or Dickie. They had the misfortune of having the seats next to my dad at the dinner table (we all had assigned seats that we had to sit in every night), Talking was not allowed at the dinner table, and I just hoped we could just get through the meal without one of us getting a beating. I remember thinking,, if I just kept my head down, eyes lowered and didn't look up or at my dad — kind of be invisible even though I was in plain sight — I might make it through dinner.

When Bert died rather unexpectedly, our lives changed greatly. My older brother, Dennis, moved to New York City at eighteen. After a visit there one weekend, I knew I could not stay in Windsor Locks, Connecticut any longer, and so at seventeen, I moved to Boston.

Living in Boston did not last long. Most of my acquaintances were a rogues gallery of gangsters, bank robbers, drug dealers (it was the 60s), and gunrunners — a very odd assortment of people who had fallen rather haphazardly into my life. When I left Boston, I hitchhiked across the country to California, California was calling me, and it was the glory days of Haight-Ashbury. It was simply time to move on, but that trip could be another whole book unto itself. If by some twist of fate my dad had not died, I would still have been in high school and probably getting ready to go to college.

Dana's great grandfather, Albert Wills, was a man of vision. Albert was a streetcar conductor in Boston, but shortly after the automobile was invented, he opened car dealerships to sell cars and garages to repair them. He was born in Maine, and after getting married, he moved to Lawrence, Massachusetts with his wife. There they raised four sons, Bert being the oldest, and the wild child. Albert had become very wealthy, and they lived quite a privileged and comfortable life. Like so many others, however, he lost the vast majority of his money and many of his possessions in the Great Depression.

Dana's maternal grandmother, Madelyn, is still alive today at 93 years old. She was raised in Lawrence, Massachusetts and worked as a schoolteacher in Hartford, Connecticut. Her father's older sisters had brought Madelyn's father, Michael O'Neil, to the United States from County Cork, Ireland. His sisters had immigrated to America as household help. Michael was an overseer in the Pacific mills wool shop for most of his life, and Dana's great grandmother, Theresa Donovan, was a stay at home mom who cared for the family and raised their five children. Her family had emigrated from Ireland to Silver Lake, Pennsylvania, where they farmed until moving to Methuen, Massachusetts.

Dana spent many years with both his grandmothers when he was growing up. Madelyn lived with us after I had packed up Dana and his sister and moved to Las Vegas, Nevada from Massachusetts. I had divorced Dana's father, I needed to get away and wanted a fresh start.

Dana's paternal grandparents were from Maine. Dana's father, the youngest of five children, was born in Bangor, Maine. His grandmother, Ilene, was a stay at home mother who never worked a day in her life. She went from living with her parents to living with her husband. She also never got a drivers license and was very dependent on others. She worried about everything to the point of obsession; I do not believe she ever enjoyed a day in her life. She would eventually develop dementia and be placed in a home where she passed away a number of years ago.

Dana's grandfather, David, worked in a factory as a machinist when they lived in Connecticut. After his retirement, they moved back to Maine, to a trailer in the woods in the middle of nowhere.

When Dana was born, David's granddaughter Joanie had been his favorite grandchild for the past five years. Now that she was going to school and not living close enough for frequent visits, David was hoping that Dana would be a girl and take her place. David and Ilene came to the hospital when Dana was born, and the only thing David said was, "You had a boy. You can keep him. We don't want him."

I was stunned. They did not even go to the nursery to see Dana. However, after making such a statement, it was strange how things would turn out between Dana and his grandfather. It took no time at all before Dana and David had quite an amazing relationship.

David was quite a character, both in physical appearance and personality. He was a small man, probably five feet, five inches tall, and he had very thin gray hair that was never combed. He usually walked around with three days worth of growth on his face. David had a very craggy, deeply wrinkled face as if he had worked out in the sun and weather all his life, and he was missing many of his teeth, which did not stop him from giving a full-on smile that revealed all those gaps between his few remaining teeth. He walked with a limp, the remnant of a stroke for which he never went to a hospital. Dana's grandmother found David on the floor one day and he could not talk or move. They did not have insurance or much money, and so she dragged him onto the couch in the living room and left him there for days. He eventually got his speech and movement back a little at a time, and the only lingering telltale sign of his stroke was the bad leg.

As Dana spent time around his grandparents, a bond between Dana and his grandfather developed. David and Ilene moved back to Maine, and we would drive up to spend a weekend. Sometimes I let Dana stay for a week with his grandfather, and the two of them would play checkers and go to the local school to see a wrestling match. Dana's grandfather had an old pickup truck that was broken down and sitting off to the side of the front yard, weeds and bushes growing up around it as it tilted off to one side on a slight hill. The windshield had a crack across it, and the paint on the body was chipped and flaking with bits of rust showing through.

Dana and his grandfather would go out and sit in that old truck, Dana in the driver's seat, and the two of them would act as if they were going places. Dana loved sitting out there in that old broken down truck that went nowhere except in a little boy's vivid imagination. Dana visited his grandparents as often as we could get up to Maine, which was a long drive from Connecticut, but when he started school it was too difficult to find the time to drive all the way up there and have to come back in a day or two. David died after a brief illness when Dana was still very young.

After spending the summer before seventh grade in Maine, Dana decided he didn't want to return to Las Vegas for school, he stayed in Maine for that school year and lived with his grandmother. All his aunts, uncles, and cousins on his father's side lived there, and Dana was close to many of them, especially one of his male cousins, Kenny, and his Aunt Bev. Bev passed away six years ago from breast cancer, a special woman who died too soon.

While living in Maine that year one of Dana's uncles bought him a horse. Dana and his sister rode his horse whenever they were visiting in Maine. Next to his grandmother's house, there was a rooster that resided in the neighbor's yard. One day Dana thought it would be funny to chase this rooster and scare it. That old rooster turned the tables on Dana. Roosters are not friendly little creatures, and unlike wild birds, they do not fly away when confronted. I was laughing the minute Dana's grandmother and uncle started telling me the story because I knew where it was going. When I was in fourth grade and my older brother, Dennis, was in sixth grade, we worked on a chicken farm. God, how I hated working there. It truly was miserable. The farmer was a mean, nasty person, and the chickens were just as mean and nasty. So I knew what Dana was in for if he was going after a rooster. The rooster that Dana thought he was going to terrorize went at him instead, and that rooster chased Dana all over the place. From that day on, every time the rooster spotted Dana outside, the bird would go after him and Dana would take off running, terrified. His uncle and grandmother told everyone the story of big bad Dana and the rooster who terrorized him, and they could not stop laughing

19

every time they told someone new the story. They said it was one of the funniest things they had ever seen.

Dana returned to Maine for part of his senior year of high school after problems in Las Vegas and graduated from Herman High School in June of 1987. I imagine he heard that story about the rooster told over and over until he left Maine after graduation.

EARLY YEARS

For the first year of Dana's life, we lived in a little, three-bedroom house in the small town of Broad Brook, Connecticut. The house was at the end of a long driveway and surrounded by dense woods. It was like a little cottage you see in storybooks. Just before you came upon the small house, there was a large white two-story home. There were stories that a crazy woman, Crazy Mary, lived in the woods out there and stalked anyone out after dark. Even grown men were afraid to be out there once night settled in.

I was a stay-at-home mom for the first year after Dana was born. In nice weather, I would take him out for walks, and in the summer I had a little plastic tub I used in the sink to wash dishes and I would fill it with water, put Dana's bathing suit on him, and take him and the tub outside in the yard to use as his own private little pool. Eventually, we bought a small blowup pool for him to sit in, the kind you can pick up at almost any store for four or five dollars. Four or five dollars back then was a lot of money to us. Dana's father only made three hundred dollars every two weeks, and our rent was three hundred dollars, which left us three hundred dollars for everything else: food, clothing, utilities, gas, diapers, etc. We did not go anywhere and we did not buy anything that was not essential.

I decided to go back to work to help with the bills, but that did not last long. I had only been working a few weeks when I got up one-morning sick to my stomach and started vomiting. All week it was the same thing, and I thought I had the flu or a stomach bug. When the nausea and vomiting extended into week two, I knew it was not the flu. I was pregnant with Dana's sister. I had to quit my job, which was fine by me. I wanted to be home taking care of Dana myself rather than having someone else with him all day.

Dana Sr. decided it was time for a change in his life and he wanted to get away from Connecticut, and so he went off to Florida with a friend to look for work. Dana and I stayed in the house in Broad Brook waiting for him to send for us once he had found a job and a place for us to live. A month later, we joined Dana Sr. in Indian Rocks Beach, Florida, and we lived there for the next nine months.

We lived one block from the beach, and every day I took Dana and his sister Kelly to the beach. I would get up and fix their breakfast, Dana would watch *Sesame Street*, and then we would head down to the beach for the rest of the morning. Around noon, we would go back to the apartment for lunch, and after lunch Dana and his sister would go down for a nap. Once the two of them were up from their naps, we would take a walk in the neighborhood and then go back to the beach until it was time for dinner, it was our daily routine.

Dana loved the ocean. He loved swimming, playing in the sand, and feeding the seagulls. Dana's love of the seaside seems strange now because one of his biggest fears is the ocean and sharks. When Dana was in his 20's he took a trip to Mexico with friends. When he returned from his trip, he told me that one afternoon they had decided to go out on one of those blow up bananas that is towed behind a small boat. The person in the boat drives so that in a very short distance and short time everyone on the banana is thrown off into the ocean. Dana said, "I hung onto that thing for dear life, there was no way in hell that guy was going to dump me in that water." He said, "I knew there were sharks out there and I wasn't going to be part of their food chain." He said, "the driver of the boat did everything he possibly could to dump me," but it just didn't happen. His friends said everyone, even people on the beach were laughing watching the scene play out, the driver of the boat doing every maneuver he could to dump Dana and Dana holding onto the banana for dear life.

When we lived in Florida, Dana liked playing in the sand, but he did not like having sand on him. He was always coming up to me at the beach asking that I brush the sand off his arms or legs. He was by no means your typical little boy who was always getting dirty. In fact, Dana was the exact opposite, always wanting to take a bath or to change his outfit, he didn't like being dirty. When he was only two years old, he would change his clothes three or four times a day.

One afternoon, he was in his bedroom and being very quiet. I peeked around the corner to see what he was doing and found that he had pulled all his clothes out of his dresser draws. Most of the clothes were on the floor and he was pulling on a pair of shorts. I asked him why he had thrown all his clothes on the floor. He told me he was trying to find something to wear (not that we were going anywhere). I told his father, "If he grows up to be gay, he is going to have the worst time with my brothers for uncles." Dana from when he was a little toddler to now, a grown man was always very fussy about his clothes and how he looked.

While living in Florida, Dana had a friend that I would hear him talking to all the time, carrying on a full-blown conversation. I asked him whom he was talking to because there was not anyone in the room with him, and he would tell me he was talking to his friend. One day I asked if his friend had a name, and he said his friend's name was Bones. I used to put the TV on while I was fixing supper and watch *Star Trek*, and I assumed that is where the name came from. It was rare that Dana ever did anything to cause trouble, but when he did something that he thought he might get into trouble for he would tell me it wasn't his fault. Bones did it.

Bones was around for quite a few months, and then I noticed Dana wasn't talking to him anymore. I asked him where Bones had been lately, and he told me he was gone. I asked him where Bones had gone, and he said, "Oh, he is dead." He completely surprised me by his answer. I didn't even think he knew what dead meant, he was only two and a half years old. I asked him a few more questions that seemed to be boring and annoying him, and so I let it go. Bones was gone forever and never did return. I wish now that I had asked Dana how Bones met his demise.

We lived on the second floor in a small two-bedroom apartment in Florida. Across the hall from us lived three boys who were deaf and attending a local college, and in the apartment below ours lived a young couple who had a little boy Dana's age. They had moved to Florida from the Midwest somewhere. The woman hated Florida and the young couple were always fighting. There was an open archway on the side of the building. That led into the backyard. Above the archway and beside it was the property owner's apartment. Once through the arch there was a large backyard. A chain link fence enclosed the entire yard, and a gate in the front yard opened to the sidewalk that led up to the house and through the archway to the backyard. The landlady and her husband, who were in their forties, were originally from Alabama, and they had a grandson who was Dana's age. Dana sometimes went to the landlord's apartment when their grandson was visiting them to play with him.

Dana had a little red tricycle that he rode up and down the sidewalk that led to the house and went under the archway to the backyard. One afternoon after we returned from the beach, I was upstairs fixing lunch and Dana was riding his bike up and down the sidewalk. One of the wheels on his bike squeaked, so I could hear the squeaking sound as he pedaled up and down the sidewalk on his bike. After only a few minutes, the squeaking stopped. I waited about a minute for it to start again, and when it didn't, I looked out the window. I could not see him in the front yard. I went downstairs and looked around the front yard. I did not see him. I then went into the backyard, and he was not there either. I hollered up to the landlady and asked her if Dana was in their apartment. She said, "No, he was in the front yard just a minute ago." My first thought twisted my stomach into a knot. I thought, oh my God, someone has taken him. Then I realized his bike was not there either. It seemed unlikely that someone would have taken his bike too. By now, the landlady had joined me in the search and was looking around the yard.

My next thought was that he had gone to the beach, which was only a block away, but he had to cross a busy street. I took off running for the beach, hoping I would find him before he crossed the street. He was not at the street and I ran across to the beach, praying he was not already at the water. Dana had a tendency at the beach to walk into the water and just keep going until he was in over his head. Once he headed into the water, I needed to be right beside him to grab him before he went too deep. When I reached the beach, he was nowhere to be seen and neither was his bike.

I ran back toward the house, where there were now four other neighbors going down the street, calling for Dana, and asking other neighbors if they'd seen him. I headed up the street in the opposite direction that everyone else was looking. A block north of us on the busy street was a small strip mall with a Laundromat, a mom and pop grocery store, and a barbershop. Next to that was a gas station and garage. As I got closer to the Laundromat, I could see that a crowd of people were standing outside. As I reached the crowd, I saw Dana in the middle of all the people. He was sitting on his bike and talking to them. He had ridden his bike to the gas station, pulled up to one of the bays, got off his bike and went inside. He asked the owner for a wrench to fix the wheel on his bike. He told the man it was squeaking and he needed to fix it. At first, the people at the garage thought it was cute, until they realized there was no adult with him. They brought Dana to the store, thinking his parents were probably there, and soon everyone in the store and Laundromat were outside asking Dana where he lived and how he got to the gas station by himself. I could not believe that was where he had gone but I was so glad to have found him safe.

Dana and I were halfway home, Dana riding his bike and I walking beside him explaining to him that he could not go places on his own without me. It was a small road we were on, more of a lane or large sidewalk than a road. It was where people who lived in a dozen little cottages drove down to park their cars next to their cottage. As I looked up from talking to Dana, I saw his father, who just happened to have come home during the search, walking down the lane towards us. I gave him a quick, little smile as an indication that all was well and Dana was fine. Instead of being relieved that Dana was found and all right, he was angry, and as soon as he reached us, he grabbed Dana by the arm, yanking him off his bike and began hitting him. I grabbed Dana Sr., to stop him from striking Dana anymore and pulled Dana away from him. No grown man should ever hit a child, especially in a fit of rage. He should have been thankful that we found Dana and that he wasn't hurt, but instead he was so mad at him for leaving the yard he was out of control.

Unfortunately, Dana's father was not Ward Clever (for those of you too young to recognize that name, he was the father on a television show, *Leave it to Beaver*). Dana's dad could not hold down a job for very long when we lived in Florida, and because of that, money was extremely tight. When he did work, there were days he would not come home, especially paydays, and by the time he showed up, most of the money from his paycheck would be gone. He would sit in the bars drinking all night and become too drunk to find his way home. He always promised it would not happen again, but he was someone for whom promises meant nothing, and obviously neither did we. There were days I would go without eating to make sure I had enough food and milk in the house for Dana and his sister. I never knew when their father would show up and if he would have any money left for groceries and rent. I certainly did not have to worry about dieting back then.

Dana's father was abusive when he drank; he was a nasty drunk, one of those people who shouldn't drink. One night before we were married, we were out with a group of friends when he became drunk and all of a sudden out of nowhere and for no apparent reason abusive. After that incident, I thought I had made it very clear to him that I would never put up with that bullshit and that would be the end of any more incidents with him. He acted as if the incident was just a onetime, crazy drunken moment and it would never happen again. I had no reason not to believe him. Unfortunately, it is true that men who are abusive do not just quit

— it only gets worse. While living in Broad Brook, Connecticut, Dana Sr. had gone out after work with some of his friends for a couple beers. I was in the kitchen feeding Dana, who was around ten months old, when his father came home. Dana Sr. came in belligerent, swearing and demanding his dinner. I fixed a plate for him and placed it on the table. He picked the plate up and threw it across the room, food flying everywhere, and hollering that he was not going to eat "the slop" I had just served him. Then out of nowhere, he punched me as hard as he could right in the jaw. I never saw it coming. I honestly was seeing stars and thought I was going to pass out. The next thing I knew, I had him up against the kitchen wall with a knife pressed against his throat. The knife was sharp and had quickly broken the skin where it came in contact with his neck making a small cut that blood was slowly beginning to trickle from. He was screaming for me to stop and get control. Once I realized what I was about to do, I slowly moved the knife away about an inch and said, "If you ever hit me in front of that baby again, I will kill you."

Dana Sr's behavior in Florida was not anything that was promising for our future. The thoughts of my children growing up in a household as I had grown up in were very disturbing to me, and I knew I could not let that happen. As parents, we always want something better for our children than we had, and I knew it was up to me to make the difference for Dana and his sister. I could not wait any longer.

Dana Sr. did not come home again one night, and I knew I had to do something to change the direction our lives were headed. I took the checkbook to the little corner grocery store and wrote a check for $300.00, I still feel guilty about that because Dana never put money in our account to cover the check. That $300.00 was the cost of two one-way plane tickets to Connecticut. I packed a bag for myself, which did not take long. I did not have many clothes living in Florida and spending so much time at the beach, a couple bathing suits, and a few pairs of shorts and couple of t-shirts. The kids had more clothes than I did, although none of us had any winter clothes. I caught a ride to the airport with a neighbor because I did not have enough money for a cab to the airport, which was quite a distance from our apartment. I was twenty-one years old and a high school dropout with two small babies, but I knew things could not stay the way they were. I was leaving Florida with my children, leaving my husband and heading toward a very unclear future.

It was December, and a blizzard was raging when I arrived in Connecticut with Dana and his sister. I grabbed a cab to my mother's house, which was only a mile away from the airport. I had not called anyone to let them know what I was doing or that I was on my way back to Connecticut. What a surprise when I walked in with my suitcase and the two babies. Three of my brothers and my sister were all still living at home. My mother, who was shocked to see us, asked, "What are you doing here?" I told her I had left Dana and I was staying there with the kids until I figured out what we were going to do next. My mother was not happy about our moving in, mostly because she was planning on coming down to Florida for a few weeks with a friend and staying with me and now my coming home had ruined her plans. My brothers, whose room I took over for the kids and I were not very happy about giving up their room to us. I took apart a bunk bed and used it as two separate beds. Dana slept in one of the beds and I had the other bed. There was a crib between the two beds for Kelly.

At the time we moved back into my mom's house, two of my brothers and most of their friends had chopped, custom motorcycles. One of their friends, Leroy, for some reason took to Dana and would come by the house if he was in the area. Every time he came over the house, he would take Dana and put him in front of him on the seat on his bike, put his shades on Dana, and slowly ride up the street. Dana would lie back against Leroy as if he was Joe cool. A number of kids were Dana's age in the neighborhood, and Dana loved it when the other kids were outside when Leroy put him on the bike. Dana would wave at the kids as they rode by, and the kids all thought it was so cool that Dana got to ride on the motorcycle. Dana always liked being the center of attention, and that has not changed much over the years.

When Dana was a toddler, I read to him all the time, especially Dr. Seuss books. By the time he was three years old, he had most of the books memorized. Dana would sometimes ask his uncles or their friends if they would like him to read a book to them. They would say yes trying to be nice to him. He would then pick up one of his books and go through it as if he were reading each page, turning to the next page at just the right time. They obviously had no idea he had memorized the books and they thought he really could read. A few of them liked to smoke so it would freak them out thinking he was only three years old reading these books. They were amazed, which pleased Dana.

I bought a record album for Dana at that time, Snoopy and the Red Baron, and for some reason, Dana absolutely loved every song on it. From the minute, he got up in the morning until I put him to bed at night, he would play that music over and over and over. I knew all the words to all the songs, and so did everyone else who lived at the house. One of my brothers said he could not take another day, another hour, or even another minute listening to it, and he hid the album. After the record was missing for a few days, Dana seemed to forget about it and my brothers were all quite happy.

In late fall, Dana was in the backyard playing and I was in the house when I heard the dog barking and barking. One of my brothers had a dog, and Dana loved playing outside with him. I could not imagine why the dog was barking so much, and I knew the neighbors would start complaining. I went into one of the bedrooms and looked out the window to see what was going on. At first, I could not see Dana or the dog. Then, as I looked toward the back of the yard that went up a hill covered with large oak trees, I saw Dana on the ground. He was lying face down with his arms over the back of his head. The barking dog was not my brother's dog but a large dog that looked like a wolf, and it was standing over Dana trying to bite his head and face. The dog was biting at his arms and pulling them away from his face and head. I freaked out, and it was as if my feet could not move fast enough to carry me out of the house, across the yard, and up the hill. As I ran through the kitchen, a broom was leaning up against the wall and without even thinking about it, I grabbed the broom as I ran past it. I headed up the hill screaming at the top of my lungs, thinking my screams would scare the dog and he would run off. That was not the case. The dog continued to attack Dana until I was almost on top of him. Just as I reached the two of them, the dog turned on me, snarling, growling, and showing his teeth. The dog continued to stand over Dana as if Dana was his prey and he was not giving him up to me. Then, without warning, he lurched into the air at me. I swung the broom so hard and so fast that beast never knew what hit him. The broomstick broke in half. The dog went flying through the air and landed on its side on the ground about three feet from us. Before the dog could get back up again, I grabbed Dana, picked him up, and ran for dear life back toward the house. I barely reached the house and got into the side door when the dog slammed right into the door as I closed it behind us.

Dana was not crying. In fact, he did not even seem scared by the whole incident, but he was confused as to why that dog was so bad and so mean. Thank God, it was cold out because Dana had on a heavy winter coat, gloves, and a hat; and although the dog had torn off the hat and one of his gloves, he seemed to be all right. I didn't notice any bite marks on his face, head, or neck, or any blood anywhere and so I thought the coat, and the fact he had his arms over the back of his neck and head, had protected him. Later that evening, when I was putting Dana in the tub for a bath, I noticed bite marks on both his arms. The dog had bitten right through his coat, shirt, and sweater and one of his ears was ripped in half. I dressed him and took him to the hospital emergency room where they had to stitch his ear back together.

Dana told me that the strange dog came into the yard and started eating the food that belonged to my brother's dog. When Dana told him no and moved toward the dog, the dog jumped on him, knocking him to the ground, and kept trying to bite him. Thank God, Dana, even at the age of four, had the good sense to turn on his stomach and try to cover his face and head. The dog was so frustrated at not being able to get to Dana's face or neck that it began barking.

Dana was not very happy with the nurses and doctors who had to stitch his ear back together. He told me he thought, "Mr. Doctor was nice, but then they hurt him." It had been a tough day all around for him. They made me leave the room while they sutured his ear, but I could hear him hollering. He kept saying, "Wait, mister! Wait a minute, Mister! Don't do that!" I felt so bad for him, although the outcome could have been much worse.

I found a babysitter for Dana and his sister during the day while I went back to school. The sitter, a friend of my mother, had six kids of her own and lived two blocks up the street from my mom's house. Kelly and her brother had become used to being together all the time, Kelly had never known a time when Dana was not with her. One weekend, I brought Dana up to his grandparents' house in Maine and left him to spend two weeks with them, but after a week, I had to bring him home because his sister was heartbroken that her brother was not around. She could not understand what had happened to him and she was too young to understand he would be coming back. In fact, after the first week that Dana was gone, the babysitter informed me she would not take Kelly until Dana returned. The entire week he was away, Kelly would not eat and all she did was cry and whimper, "Dane, I want brother." There was no consoling her and it was painful to watch. Dana and his sister were inseparable when they were younger, and even from a young age he was very protective of her. It was sad to see that change, as they got older.

We lived at my mother's house for a year and a half while I went to school to become a licensed practical nurse. When I graduated, I got a job working at Mt. Sinai Hospital in Hartford, Connecticut and began searching for a house. The only home I could afford was in a small town called Ware in western Massachusetts. I had never even heard of this town when I saw an ad in the *Hartford Courant* for "affordable townhouses" there. It was an hour and a half drive from my job, but at least we would have our own place. I ended up buying a brand new two story, three bedroom, one and a half bath townhouse in a development called Warebrook Village. Now, after a year and a half of all three of us in one bedroom, we all had our own bedrooms.

Ware was a great little Norman Rockwell town in the middle of Massachusetts. It had the quaint little Main Street with mom and pop stores, a couple of churches, big brick mill factories next to the river that ran through the town, and an old granary building that was turned into a restaurant. Dana started school there, played peewee football and little league baseball, took karate and trombone lessons, and was in the cub scouts. He also took swimming lessons at the town pool right around the corner from our house, and in the winter he skated with his friends on the field next to the pool and up at a pond in the woods that the kids called Witch's Pond. After a snowstorm, Dana and his sister would spend hours sledding down the big hill in front of our house with all the other kids who lived in the Village. Dana's life was in fact very typical of all little boys' lives in rural Massachusetts.

I bought a dog, a boxer pup named Swizzle — the people I bought the dog from had given her that name. She was one of the best, smartest, most protective dogs ever, and Dana used to sneak her into his bed with him in spite of the fact that she was not allowed on the furniture. Even when he was in high school, he still had her sleep in his bed. I just happened to be looking out the kitchen window one day when I was home from work, and I saw Dana walking down the street toward the house with Swizzle walking beside him. Three older boys came up behind Dana and started talking to him, then one of the boys grabbed Dana by the shirt and threw him against a chain link fence they were standing next to. I started out the front door to stop the boys from whatever it was they were up to, but in the few seconds it took me to open the door and step outside, Swizzle had the three boys pinned up against the fence, barking and snarling at them. She was very vicious looking when she would lower her head, roll her lips, showing her canines, and begin with a menacing low growl. The three boys were begging Dana to call off his dog. Dana told Swizzle to stop, and the two of them walked off side by side to the house. Dana was so excited that Swizzle had come to his rescue he could not wait to tell me how she had just saved him from these three older boys. I did not let him know I had seen the whole thing. Those boys never bothered Dana again, and word spread throughout this small town that Dana had a dog that would attack you if you bothered Dana. Dana never again had any bullies or older kids bother him for the seven years we lived in Ware.

There was an incident with Dana one day that reminds me of a Mark Twain story, probably because it involves a raft, in a river, in a small town and a group of young boys. Two brothers who lived about eight houses up the street from us were, 13 and 14 years old, and a couple of smartasses. Dana was only eight, but he loved it when they would play with him or let him hang out with them. They were always nice to him and so I didn't object.

One afternoon, Dana asked if he could go to the pool with the two brothers, they weren't going swimming; they were just going to hang out. I told the boys to be sure they watched Dana and that I did not want them gone too late. They assured me he would be safe and back soon, but Dana did not get home until late that afternoon and the boys did not come in the house with him. I was mad that he was gone so long and they had not gotten him home earlier, but Dana told me they could not get home any sooner. He proceeded to tell me that the boys met up with two more of their friends, two boys I did not like, and they did not go to the pool but instead went to the woods down by the river. They had a blowup raft, which they put in the water, then held it and had Dana get in it. The boys had told Dana they were going to get in with him, but then they let it go with just him in the raft. As Dana's story went on, I was getting madder and madder. Dana proceeded to tell me the water started moving the raft down the river very fast and the older boys started running next to the river trying to keep up with the raft and hollering at Dana to hold on. Finally, one of the brothers jumped into the river and grabbed onto the raft, trying to pull the raft back over to the edge of the river. Dana told me it took the boy a long time to get the raft back to shore, where the rest of the boys were still running to keep up with the raft. They were hollering for the older boy to swim hard. When he was finally able to get the raft close to the riverbank, the second brother jumped into the river to help get Dana back on the bank and off the raft. They then had to walk all the way back to town, and that was why Dana was late getting home.

I was more than mad now and headed straight for the two boys' house that were to have taken my son to the swimming pool. The boys got an ear full and their parents told what they had done. Apparently, putting this little kid in the raft and letting it loose was supposed to be a joke. They thought Dana would get scared when they let him go on the raft by himself, and it would be very funny, but it all quickly backfired. They were the ones who got scared when the current started moving the raft down the river a lot faster than what they were expecting. After that, Dana was no longer allowed to go with the brothers anymore, and their parents grounded both of them for a long time. Dana did not realize that the boys did something that was mean and dangerous. He thought it was great when one of the brothers jumped into the river to help him.

Dana's first little league game was in Ware. We were all there to watch him, the whole family. All my brothers were (and still are) huge sports fans: baseball, football, basketball, boxing, and karate. They especially followed all the Boston teams. My brother George had a black belt in Tae Kwon Do that he had received while a Green Beret in Laos during the Vietnam War, and he taught Tae Kwon Do when he first returned to the states.

I was the only one out of six of us in the family who had children at the time, and for seven years, Dana, and his sister were the only niece and nephew. Our family was always very close, and so everyone in the family came to all of Dana and Kelly's events. We also spent Thanksgiving, Christmas, and Fourth of July together; and we had family reunions every other year, even though at times we were spread out across the country. We would have cookouts at each other's houses, and when one of us would rent a cottage at

Hampton Beach, we always rented one with as many bedrooms as we could get because we knew all the family and our friends would be coming up. The beach was always great fun and a big part of all our lives. When my brothers, sister, and I were little kids, my dad would save all year so we could go on a two-week vacation to the beach. The tradition continued with all our kids, Dana and his sister and their cousins, and it continues to this day with our grandchildren. There were enough of us when we were older and had children that we had two full teams for our wiffle ball games on the beach. Usually, the games were at the end of a day spent at the beach or on a cloudy, cool day. When Dana got older, he always wanted to be one of the captains, and my brother Dickie would be the other captain. The two would argue over every call, and then spend the rest of the night arguing over every play of the game, the loser always saying that their team would have won except for a bad call.

Two of my brothers, Dickie and Michael, were the kings of making sand castles. They would spend endless hours making a sand castle with Dana and Kelly when they were younger. Of course, the sand castle always had to be close enough to the water, at low tide, so as the tide came in it would crash through the walls that surrounded the main castle and fill moats until nothing was left of their hours of work. I don't know why, but that was always the best part of making the sand castles, watching the waves turn them back to just sand on the beach. Then there was always a night at Brown's Lobster Pound for steamers, lobsters, and fish and chips; and you couldn't keep the family away from the arcades at night, especially Dana. The older he got, the more he could not wait to go to the arcade, and when I say older I am talking twenty and thirty and thirty-five years of age.

When Dana played in his first little league baseball game, the whole family was there to watch him. Dana was out in left field and looked so tiny standing out there. His uniform was too big for him. The shirt came down to his knees and the pants hung down onto his sneakers. After being on the field for only a few minutes, I saw two men talking to him. I went down to the field to see what was going on. They asked me how old he was and I told them he was six and would be seven in July. They said he was young and small for his age and maybe I should consider taking him out of little league until next year. I told them no, that he was old enough and had tried out to be on a team, that he had been chosen to be on this team and he was staying.

Most little boys at that age get bored playing in the outfield and do not pay a whole lot of attention to the game, and Dana was no exception. At the very beginning of the game, the boy who was up at bat cracked the ball high into the air and it was heading right into left field where Dana was standing. We were all on our feet as the ball headed directly to Dana, who did not have to move an inch to catch the ball. He just had to put his glove out and the ball would fall right into it. What a surprise when Dana just stood perfectly still and the ball fell right at his feet. Everyone was screaming and hollering for Dana to pick up the ball as the batter ran around the bases. Two of his uncles were running around the outside of the fence toward Dana hollering for him to pick up the ball and throw it. Dana just stood there looking around, trying to figure out what all the screaming and hollering was about. Every adult at the game was screaming and hollering, either for Dana to pick up the ball or for the batter to keep running. The batter did keep running and Dana did not pick up the ball. The batter got an inside-the-park homerun.

Dana went to all of his practices and to the games every week. His coach was a nice guy who took all the boys out for ice cream after each game, and win or lose; he told them all what a great job they had done. Dana was lucky to have this man as his coach because some of the other coaches were all about winning and not the kids having fun.

In those days, (the seventies), there was no t-ball; the boys pitched to each other. At the very beginning of the season, Dana was hit by a pitch and was afraid to get too close to the plate after that. Every time he got up to bat, he would strike out. Many times, he did not even swing at a single pitch. Even though he was not a very good baseball player, the kids all liked Dana, who was very sweet and friendly. I would always tell him he did good, that he almost hit the ball when he did swing at it, and that next time I was sure he would hit it. In fact, the last game of the season, during his last time up at bat with two strikes against him, it was like a Red Sox moment — he swung and hit the ball. Not only did he hit the ball but he made it safe to first base. Every parent at the game, including the parents of members of the other team, were on their feet cheering for him. One woman who was with the opposing team asked one of the other moms why they were all clapping and hollering for Dana on the opposing team, and she said, "He's played every game and never got a hit before." The next year he played little league again but improved only slightly.

Dana also played peewee football and was again small compared to some of the other kids. His uniform was too big, and when he put his helmet on, he looked like a little bobble-head running around on the field. I never had to push him to go, and I never remember him telling me he did not want to go, but rather, he faithfully went to all his football practices and to every game.

On Sunday mornings, I liked to get up before Dana and his sister and I would put cinnamon buns in the oven. The Pillsbury ones you can buy at the grocery store, nothing homemade but they still smelled and tasted great, I'm sure better than if I had made them from scratch. When Dana and Kelly woke up, the smell of the cinnamon buns would be wafting through the whole house. They both loved those sweet, sticky baked buns, and I always loved the idea of waking to the smell of something baking in the oven and of having warm memories of Sunday morning at home. I used to love Sunday mornings. We attended the local Catholic Church in Ware and Dana became an altar boy. Dana was in fact one of the altar boys for his sister's first communion. I wish I had written down some of the stories he would tell me when he came home from his catechism classes. Dana would reiterate the story they had taught in class, like Jesus and the five loaves of bread and fishes, then he would give me his take on the story. Of course, his interpretation was never anywhere close to what the real meaning of the story was, but his take on it was funny to hear.

When I made the decision to move to Las Vegas, Dana told the priest at the parish he would not be able to assist at mass anymore. The priest was quite upset and asked if I could come in for a meeting with him. At our meeting, he told me he was upset about Dana moving away, that Dana was very inquisitive about God and the teachings of the Catholic Church and he felt that, with the right encouragement and direction, Dana might be destined for the priesthood. I am sure, if that priest has passed on, he is turning over in his grave to see the direction Dana took, and the person he has become.

Knowing Dana now, it is hard to believe; but when Dana was younger, he did not like to fight and he did not like other kids being picked on. It was the sixties and seventies, and my friends and I were pacifists (make love, not war), and it seems Dana was following our lead. In his school picture from kindergarten, he has cuts and scabs on the bridge of his nose and on both of his lips. The one on his nose was from another little boy cracking Dana across the face with a metal shovel when Dana tried to stop this boy from beating up another boy at the playground next to our house. The busted up lips happened when Dana was on a slide at school and another little boy climbed up and got in front of the child who was waiting his turn to go down the slide. Dana told the boy who was cutting in front of the other child he could not do that and he had to wait for his turn. The boy turned to Dana and pushed him off the ladder, sending him to the ground below landing on his face. Dana was my little hero, always trying to step up to the plate to help someone else.

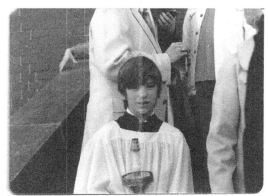

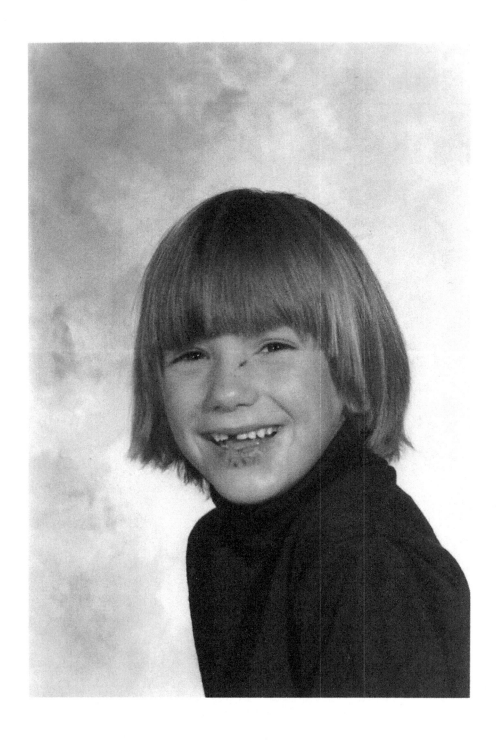

EDUCATION

Considering what Dana has done with the UFC and how he deals with contracts, fighters, managers, lawyers, politicians, boxing commissions, television deals, cable and on and on, you would think that he did extremely well in school. That was not the case. Dana was bright, but trying to get him to apply himself was another thing. I believe that the education you receive in the early years, well before college, is the most important (not that Dana ever went to college — more of the myth). Early education is the foundation for everything else; if you cannot read or write then your future will not be very bright. I tried very hard to stay on top of what was going on with Dana in school. When we went out to eat, I would always ask Dana to figure out the tip for me. You cannot believe how difficult that was for him well into his high school years. I would tell him, "Take the billed amount, move the decimal point over one place, and then just double the amount. So if the bill is $20.00, move the decimal point over one place, which would be $2.00, and then just double that. So $2.00 plus $2.00 is $4.00, and that will be the tip." It was something that seemed so simple, but he just could not wrap his head around it. Half the time he would get frustrated and just start guessing at what he thought the tip should be. I am sure Dana has no problems figuring out math, especially with money, these days, just using much bigger numbers.

Dana started school while we were living in Ware, Massachusetts. In 1974, he was in kindergarten, and his report card shows he did very well, especially in recitation. His teacher's comments for his first semester were, "Dana has adjusted quite well to school, both socially and academically. He's a good pupil and works hard at whatever he does." His teachers were always stating how Dana worked hard at everything he tried to do.

In second grade, Dana began having problems in the classroom. On February 11, 1977, I had a meeting with the school psychologist, classroom teacher, special services teacher, and the speech pathologist. Dana went through a battery of tests, and now that we had the results, we needed to decide what actions, if any, needed to be taken. Dana's I.Q. test indicated that he was in the bright normal category at 112, but there was a twenty point I.Q. difference between his verbal score (120) and his performance (100). Other tests indicated that he was having trouble remembering what he heard or saw and then writing it down on paper. If he were shown a flash card that said "the little white house," he might write "house white the little." He was not dyslexic, but he was definitely having serious problems that needed to be addressed quickly and aggressively. A special program was set up for him. He would leave his class three times a week for thirty minutes every day to work with a special education teacher for the remainder of second grade and all of third grade. All the work of the special education teacher and his regular teachers paid off, and he was able to overcome his learning problem. His second grade teacher wrote, "Dana is a hard working boy. He tries very hard to do good work. I'm pleased with his progress."

I think it was his second grade teacher he had a crush on. She was young, pretty, and drove a sports car. Dana would try very hard to do well in her class because then he got to stay after school and help her erase the chalkboards and do other chores. She called me one day and asked if it would be all right if she took Dana to Friendly's for a soda and then she would bring him home. I thought he was going to burst when she pulled up at our house in front of all the other kids in her sports car. She had discovered Dana liked attention and would act out and try to be funny in class or get in trouble to get it. She turned the tables. She only gave him attention if he was good or worked hard. When he realized he was not getting any attention for misbehaving in her class, he did a complete turnaround. She had his number early on.

There was a story he had written in her class about a monkey who gets on a rocket ship and goes to the moon. He had drawn pictures to go with the words and put it all together in a book form with a picture of a monkey sitting on a rocket ship and the moon in the background as the cover. I kept it, and about six years ago, I gave it to Dana's wife. She is not apparently very sentimental, and I am sure it is in a landfill now.

In fourth grade, Dana was struggling again and had fallen a year behind in math. He would struggle with math from that point on, although again, I am sure he is very good at math now. You cannot deal with the sums of money he does and not be good with numbers.

When Dana was in fifth grade, we moved to Las Vegas, Nevada. I applied to nursing school while we lived in Ware, Massachusetts and was accepted. I attended school fulltime and worked fulltime. After two years of school, I received my degree in science and was able to take the exams to become a registered nurse. Dana Sr. had been in and out of our lives since I had left him in Florida. I knew he was never going to change and be the husband or father we needed, and so I made it final and filed for divorce. Dana's father would not let me get on with my life, however, and so after graduating with my nursing degree I decided it would be best to start over somewhere else. In April of 1980, off to Las Vegas we went. Las Vegas was a small town back then. They had just put traffic lights in and UNLV was in the middle of the desert. At a bar a few blocks from our house, men still rode their horses to the bar and tied them to a post out front. The Strip was made up of some small hotels — the Sands, the Dunes, the Sahara, and a few others — and there were vast areas of desert between them.

Dana finished fifth grade at Gene Ward Elementary in Las Vegas, but sixth grade was a problem. When I received his report card, I found out he had been absent from school for twenty-plus days. I was furious with both Dana and the school. Dana would leave everyday as if he were going to school but never get on the bus. The school never called me to let me know he was not showing up for school day after day. When I called about his absences, unbelievably their response was, "It's not our job to keep track of your son." I was even more furious with Dana than with the school administrators for thinking he was going to get away with it. I had very few rules in my house, but the big one was, "Do Not Lie to Me!" Acting as if he was going to school every day and then not attending was indeed a lie, and I told him I was going to put him in Catholic school to solve this problem. The nuns would take care of him and there would be no more missing school once he was with them. Although this was mostly an idle threat because most of Catholic schools no longer had nuns teaching the classes, but he didn't know that.

Dana went to his grandmother's in Maine for that summer. When it came time for him to return to Las Vegas for school, he told me he did not want to come back. He said he wanted to stay in Maine with his cousins and grandmother and go to school there. At first, I said no, but then I thought he was just testing me and, after a semester in Maine, he would want to come home. I let him stay; he stayed for the full year but returned to Las Vegas for eighth grade. When he started eighth grade, he went to Saint Viator's Catholic school. The nuns now had him, but unfortunately, there were very few nuns still teaching at St. Viators.

Mobil

Dear Mom,

Hi. How are you I'm fine. I'm Having a pretty good time. you should see how big david is. He's 6'2. I miss you a lot. Do you know what uncle Glenn boughtme a horse her name is Lady she's the sweetest little thing. Today gram jeanie l.kenny and I. have to go sighn up for school grams afraid there going to give her a hard time & I dont know why? Mom l. kenny cleaned out his drawers and gave me two of them. Oh ya I loved your birthday card thanck you. Mom I just got back from getting registered You see I started writing this letter this morning but then I wanted you to see about event at school. you know what I mean. Well anyway. we went down to the school and it wasn't open but the janitor said they would open a week before school starts well I gues it to be going Mom, bye bye

Love

ya Dana xxoo

When Dana attended Carvel Junior High School in Maine, his grades were good: Grammar 73, Spelling 84, Math 70, Science 80, Social Studies 90, Reading 87, P.E. 95, Health 93, Music B. But Dana's first report card from St. Viator's was a disaster: Knowledge of Catholic Doctrine C, Reading D, Comprehension needs improvement, Word Knowledge needs improvement, Effort in Class needs improvement, Math C, English satisfactory, Grammar Skills failed, Written Expression needs improvement, Spelling D, Science failed, Social Studies C, Penmanship needs improvement, Art satisfactory, Music C. Yet when tested by the school when he first applied, to determine where he was academically on the SRA Achievement Series, he scored mostly at or above the national average, which meant he was not even trying. He soon began to like school life at St. Viator's, however, and the following year, moved on to Bishop Gorman High School, where he attended with his current UFC partner Lorenzo Fertitta.

Most of the kids Dana went to school with at Gorman came from wealthy families. I was working anywhere from eight to twenty-four hours a day seven days a week to pay for school and the mortgage and the day to day bills, and so I didn't have a lot of free time or extra money. Dana's father never paid his child support or provided health insurance for Dana or Kelly as was agreed to in the divorce decree. It was nice that Dana's friends at Gorman had second homes in places like Coronado, California; Park City and Brian Head, Utah; and other places where the rich apparently congregate. Dana was always being invited to go skiing or to the beach with his friends' families. I never asked Dana to work while he was in high school, and so it was easy for him to go places with his friends when he was invited. Dana joined the ski club at Gorman, and for Christmas that year, I bought him skis, bindings, boots, and all the clothes he needed to go skiing. Previously, he had to rent everything, and all his friends had their own skis, boots, and other equipment, which embarrassed Dana.

Dana liked going to these places and seeing all the nice things money could buy. I thought these trips a good lesson and hoped he would see that, if he worked hard and was good at what he did, then there was reward at the end. I also thought that having rich, powerful friends does not hurt either. I always told Dana, "I don't care what you choose to do in life, but make sure you're the best at it. Do it one hundred percent. Do not just be mediocre or put your time in everyday."

Gorman High School expelled Dana not once, but twice. Someone recently asked me why the school expelled him and I really couldn't remember. It took very little to be thrown out of Gorman. I believe the first time was for cutting school. After he was expelled from Gorman, he went to Las Vegas High School, which Dana hated. He told me every day that he wanted to go back to Gorman. Some of the boys at Las Vegas High School terrorized Dana. When he was at Gorman, Dana and his friends had started fights with some of the students at Las Vegas High School, now these boys were thrilled to see Dana at their school. He would do anything he could to avoid these boys, and every day they let him know they were going to kick his ass. It took a lot of begging on my part to get him back into Gorman High School, but he didn't seem to learn a lesson from the first time, he was soon expelled again.

I was having problems with him at home too. The last straw was when he got into a car accident driving his girlfriend's grandparents' car. Dana was at a party and had been drinking. One of the girls he went to school with asked him for a ride home. He said he would give her a ride home, a bad decision obviously, and lost control of the car. Both of them were thrown from the car, but luckily, his passenger only had a cut on her thigh and Dana escaped with contused kidneys, cuts, and bruises. He was lucky he escaped with such few injuries, because he went through the windshield.

When Dana was released from the hospital, I sent him back to Maine to finish high school. He had again broken one of my few rules: never drink and drive or get in a car with someone who has been drinking. I worked in the recovery room and frequently saw the results of kids drinking and driving. Dana and his sister were told they were to stay where they were or call me or someone else to pick them up. Dana had once told me I had taken all the fun out of drinking for him after telling him he could drink as long as he was sensible about it, which meant no drinking and driving, no leaving the place you where at once you started drinking.

While Dana was in Maine for his senior year, he called to tell me he wanted to come home for Thanksgiving and Christmas. He told me to buy him a plane ticket so he could be home for the longest amount of time and be with his friends. I was annoyed and hurt that he did not ask me if I had the money to buy him a plane ticket, but rather, demanded this be done for him. I was also annoyed and hurt that he did not care about spending the holidays with his family, but instead he wanted to hang out with friends over the holidays. Christmas and Thanksgiving were always a big deal at our house, and he could have cared less about being with his family. I decided he could come home for Thanksgiving and Christmas but he would be traveling by bus. It was to take three days, traveling day and night.

However, things did not turn out as planned, and the trip was certainly an experience of a lifetime for Dana. Dana did not get home until after the Thanksgiving holiday and had to go back to Maine after a very, very short stay in Vegas. At major bus stops, he would call me to let me know where he was and how things were going. In Detroit, he called me to inform me he had to go to the bathroom but the clientele that were at that bus station were suspect at best and he could not bring himself to go into the bathroom. I asked, "What do you think I can do?"

He said, "I don't know, but I thought you might think of something."

It was in Detroit that he got on the wrong bus and, instead of heading for Las Vegas, ended up in Wyoming. I was at the bus station in Vegas waiting for his bus when he called to tell me he made a mistake at one of the bus stops and got back on the wrong bus. I had to buy another ticket to get him to Vegas, and it took another whole day of traveling for him to arrive. For the Christmas holiday, I bought him a plane ticket, but I think the cross-country bus trip was really an eye opening experience for him.

At the time he transferred to Hermon High School, Dana had enough credits from Gorman that he only needed to take three classes. He graduated from Hermon High School in Bangor, Maine in June of 1987. I had finally gotten him through high school. His sister Kelly, his girlfriend Jenny Wynn, his Uncle Richard and Aunt Michele and their daughter Jessica, and his grandmother and I all went to Bangor for his graduation. Dana returned to Las Vegas after the graduation.

LAS VEGAS

My mother, Dana, Kelly and I, and our two boxer dogs, Swizzle and Bowzer, were all loaded into the car for our move across the country. Every day before I started driving, I gave Dana and one of the dogs a Dramamine because they both would get carsick. About an hour after giving them both the pill, I would look in the rear view mirror and see the two of them leaning against each other, propping each other up, their heads nodding and their eyes fluttering slowly shut.

My car was an older Mercury Monarch and I was towing a 1958 MG that I was attempting to restore. On top of the car was a container holding our luggage for the trip. It was quite the adventure driving across the country. It was funny because I thought it would be educational and a great learning experience for Dana and his sister, but it's a long trip, and soon after our trip began, all I really wanted to do was get there — never mind all the places we could stop along the way and play tourist. The weather was not about to co-operate with my idea of a pleasant cross-country drive either. In Ohio, Indiana, and Illinois we ran into severe weather, including tornadoes. The rain was coming down so hard and fast at one point the motor for the windshield wipers burned out. We had to pull off the highway and spend the night and much of the next day in a motel next to the highway while a local garage ordered and replaced the windshield wiper motor. A tractor-trailer truck traveling in front of us on the highway was blown off the road by strong winds and rolled over into a ditch. In Texas, an emergency alert interrupted the radio station I was listening to telling people to take cover because sand and flying rock storm was moving quickly toward some road. I didn't even know what highway we were on, but of course, it was heading towards us. As I looked to the south, all I could see was this wall of dark brown that was easily seventy-five to eighty feet high and stretched as far as the eye could see and it was moving in our direction. There was nothing but open space all around us and no place to take cover. We had to out run the sand storm, which looked like something out of the movie *The Mummy*. I had the gas pedal floored until I finally thought we were safe from the elements as we drove up into the mountains of Arizona. It was April and winter was over, or so I thought. We drove straight into a raging blizzard. The car was so weighted down with luggage, passengers, and the car I was towing that tractor-trailer trucks were passing us as we drove up into the mountains. I had the gas pedal floored again, but we were only going fifteen miles an hour and I was afraid we were going to start sliding backward down the mountain. I was white knuckled all the way to the desert of Arizona.

We stopped at a tourist store in the middle-of-nowhere Texas, (this was Texas 30 years ago) that had all kinds of cowboy and Indian souvenirs. Dana was excited about moving to Las Vegas, thinking it would be full of cowboys and Indians. When he saw all the items in this store, he just had to have this packet that contained a leather Indian headband, a half inch leather piece with some beading that went around a person's bicep and a painted wooden tomahawk rounded out the contents of the package. The armband had two leather strands that hung approximately six inches from the main arm piece and attached to the ends of the leather strands were a couple of white feathers. He was so excited when I relented to his pleas and purchased the packet for him.

When we arrived in Las Vegas, we were very much like many of the tourists there. We had never seen any of the sights or casinos, and so we headed downtown to Fremont Street one night to see the casinos and the lights. Dana was excited about going out because he wanted to wear his new Indian pieces, and believe me there was no talking him out of it. Why squash childhood imagination or kill what might make for great memories? Dana walked around downtown with no shirt on, barefoot, his wooden tomahawk stuck in the loop of his jeans, and his head band and arm band in place. Everyone was turning and staring at him as we walked by and he thought it was because he looked so cool. I did not have the heart to tell him otherwise. Welcome to Vegas, Indian Dana.

When we finally reached Las Vegas and the house, I had rented, the movers had not yet delivered the furniture, (it was supposed to be there the week before we arrived) and the realtor had not maintained the yard. The grass was brown and dead and the pool looked like a black swamp. I was waiting for the swamp creature to come crawling out of it. I went to the nearby drug store and bought four folding lawn chairs that I, Dana, his sister, and their grandmother all slept on until the furniture arrived three weeks late. I did not have enough money left after our cross-country trip to go to a hotel, so sleeping in the living room on these lawn chairs had to do. I was starting work that week at Valley Hospital, and so I needed to stretch the last of my money until I got my first pay-check. The hospital did not pay every week when I first started, but every two weeks, and worse yet, I did not know they held back your first paycheck. I was counting out pennies before I received my first pay. It took no time at all for Dana and Kelly to make friends with all the kids in the neighborhood, and once our furniture arrived and I was able to get the pool clean, our house quickly became the neighborhood place where all the other kids came to play and swim.

From 1980, when we first moved to Las Vegas, until 1986, Dana's grandmother would come out in October and spend the winters with us. This worked out well for all of us because I was a single mother working eighty to a hundred hours a week as a nurse to support Dana and his sister. When Dana attended St. Viator's, which was quite a distance from our house; his grandmother drove him to school and picked him up every day. When Dana and Kelly got out of school, their grandmother would be at the house waiting for them. She fixed supper every night for them and made sure they did their homework. We were not in Las Vegas for very long when I received a phone call from my youngest brother, Michael. He proceeds to tell me he is on his way to Las Vegas, his car broke down, they were in Missouri somewhere and he didn't have the money to fix it, and yes he did say, they. I sent him the money he needed by Western Union, and a few days later he showed up on my doorstep. Michael, his girlfriend and their 2-year-old son with no money and the only person they knew in Vegas was me. They moved in with us until Michael and his girlfriend found jobs and saved up enough money to get their own apartment.

Dana and his sister, for the longest time were either sharing their bedrooms with someone or giving up their bedrooms altogether to visitors. The rented house only had three bedrooms so there were times the house was full of people. Another one of my brothers, George, lost his job in Connecticut. He had run out of money and didn't know what he was going to do. I bought him a plane ticket to come out to Vegas and he moved in with us, staying for three years while he got back on his feet. My sister, Frances, showed up on my doorstep one night after we had been living in Vegas for a couple years, pregnant and with her boyfriend. No phone call, no notice just rang my doorbell one night and said hi, I'm moving out here. They moved in with us until her boyfriend found a job and they were able to get their own place. At least by the time my sister joined us I had bought a five-bedroom house. With all the company and family staying with us, we needed the five bedrooms. Living in Las Vegas people were always coming out to visit for a week or two, not that I minded. It was always nice to have a house full of people.

In the summer when school let out, Dana and Kelly would go back East. That way I didn't have to worry about them being home with babysitters or, when they got older, alone while I was at work, which was all the time. Kelly would spend the majority of her summer with her grandmother in Wales, Massachusetts, and Dana the majority of his summer in Levant, Maine with his other grandmother. They both had many friends and relatives back east, so they looked forward to seeing everyone and escaping the brutal, Las Vegas summers.

One evening while I was at work, my brothers, George and Michael decided they were going to take a ride out to a place on the Colorado River known as the hot springs. They took Dana with them without calling me. Dana was probably twelve years old at the time. It is part of our family mythology that anyone who goes anywhere with my brother George always has a story to tell for life, and that was the case for Dana on this occasion. Around nine-thirty that night, I receive a call at work from my brother Michael. He asks if I have heard from Dana or George. I had no idea why he was asking because I assumed Dana and George were at home. Michael explained that the three of them went to the hot springs for the afternoon. It's not the easiest place to get to, to reach the hot springs you have to hike down cliffs. Michael says to me that, on the way back up to the car, he ran ahead of George and Dana. After he climbed up the rope that hangs down over a small cliff area, he pulled the rope up so they couldn't get to the car. He apparently thought this would be funny.

Michael said he waited for George and Dana to reach the cliff where the rope had been hanging, but they never showed. When it started getting dark, he walked back to the car thinking that maybe they hiked out another way. As I am listening to his story, I could not believe Dana was in the desert somewhere lost and it was now dark. I left work and drove out toward Boulder Dam. Just as you pass a small casino before the dam, you have to drive off the road down a steep hill into the desert. If you have never been in the desert at night, let me tell you it is so black out there, you can't see two feet in front of you, and it is creepy. You feel that any minute some maniac is going to jump out in front of you with some implement of dismemberment like in slasher movies. Just sitting in the desert by myself in the dark was freaking me out; my nerves were beginning to get the better of me. The only light was the beams coming from my headlights and that only went two or three feet before being completely swallowed up by the dark, desert night. You couldn't see an inch further and the desert was eerily quiet. I waited for half an hour, I was just getting ready to leave when Michael walked out of the blackness and into the beam from my headlights. My heart skipped about ten beats when I first saw this figure appear just feet in front of my car, I didn't realize it was him right away. It was now after ten o'clock, and George and Dana still had not showed up.

After waiting another thirty minutes, I was getting ready to go to the police and report the two of them missing and lost in the desert, when they both walked into the beams of light coming from my car. George had seen Michael pull the rope up and thought they could go around a different way, but in the desert, things that look close are really a long way off. It began to get dark and they had no idea where they were. At one point, they were at the top of what George thought was a small rock outcropping that they needed to climb down. George told Dana he would go first and then Dana could climb down after him into this pitch black hole. George climbed over some rocks and started his decent down the cliff wall, within moments he lost his footing and fell ten or fifteen feet onto the ground below. He landed on his back with a thud, and landed so hard that the fall knocked the wind out of him; he could not move or speak. Dana heard him fall but could not see him, and began calling out to George. George could not answer him, Dana thought his uncle was dead and he was in the middle of the desert in the middle of the night now all by himself. He was terrified.

After a few minutes, George caught his breath and was able to call up to Dana telling him to lower himself over the edge and start climbing down the rocks. As Dana began to climb over the rocks and down the cliff, George lit his towel on fire so Dana could see where he was going. I don't know how they were able to find their way from that point, but they did. I was so mad at my brothers for dragging Dana out there without calling me, I was ready to kill both of them.

As Dana's sixteenth birthday approached, he came to me and asked what kind of car I would be buying for him for his birthday. He said, "All the kids at school were getting beamers or SUVs." I told him, "I can't buy one of those for myself, never mind for you." I said, "You will not be getting a car of any variety from me." After a few days, I felt bad because turning sixteen seemed to be such a big deal for all his friends. I caved in and handed him two thousand dollars and told him that was the best I could do. I'm not sure how it happened, but Dana did end up getting a car, an old used Jeep. It looked like an old army jeep. I found out later that someone forged my name as a co-signer to the loan papers. Dana swore it was not him. Dana and his friends immediately named the car "The Beast."

Dana did not have The Beast for long. The Beast turned out to be a nightmare. A few days after getting, the Beast, Dana was driving over to a friend's house; another school friend was riding with him in the passenger's seat. Dana made a right turn and his passenger was nearly ejected from the jeep. It took everything for him to grab onto the roll bar and hang on for dear life. The seat was not bolted to the floor, it wasn't attached to anything. The next day Dana drove The Beast to a friend's house, when he arrived and turned the car off; he realized smoke was coming from under the hood. The engine was on fire and the fire department had to respond.

The Jeep was still drivable and the following day we took the Beast back to the car lot where Dana had purchased it. I told the owner of the car lot that he needed to take care of all the problems with the car or return Dana's money. The owner told us to leave the Jeep and he would see that the problems were addressed. The dealer never repaired anything on the jeep and then refused to return Dana's money. Dana ended up with no car and no two thousand dollars, which he had used for the down payment on the jeep, and he still had the bank loan on the car. If nothing else, I can only say it was a lesson in dealing with individuals who have no principles or ethics. I discovered much to my dismay there was very little we could do, but I'm one of those people who believe in karma, what comes around goes around. We did find out that the car dealer who ripped Dana off was arrested for selling cocaine a year later and went to jail for a very long time.

I decided while Dana was still in high school that I would give him his own American Express card for emergencies and with it teach him a little responsibility. I made sure he knew it was only to be used for emergencies. The following month I receive my bill from American Express with $1,800 in charges on it that were not mine. I had problems with my American Express bill with charges in the past so I put a call into American Express to explain there were charges on my bill that did not belong to me. It never even occurred to me that it could have been Dana. I had just given him the card. A ring and bracelet were charged that had been purchased at a jewelry store, and there were a couple of restaurant charges. The person on the phone asked me if I knew a Dana White. They then informed me all the receipts were signed by Dana White. Dana hadn't had the card but a couple of days when he went out and bought jewelry for his girlfriend and was taking his friends out to lunch and putting it all on his credit card. So much for emergencies and responsibility, I don't know what I was thinking. When Dana came home, I asked him how he planned to pay for everything he had charged to the American Express card since he was not working and had no job prospects. He stated he didn't think about paying when he was using the card. The card was taken away from him.

Dana and his sister were very close when they were young. He always watched out for her. In high school, however, they did not get along very well and were constantly fighting. Kelly entered Bishop Gorman High School in ninth grade, and Dana was two years ahead of her. There was an incident soon after Kelly arrived at Bishop Gorman. I received a phone call at work one day from Dana. He informed me I would probably receive a phone call from the police letting me know he had been arrested and was in jail. I asked him why he thought he was about to be arrested. He explained he was on his way to the grocery store to beat the hell out of a boy from Gorman who was working there. I asked him, what brought this about. He said the boy had seen Kelly at the school football game on Friday night and offered her a ride to the dance after the game. Gorman always had a dance for all the kids who attended Gorman after the football games at Ryan Hall at the school. She had told him she was with friends and did not need a ride. Apparently, this boy the following Monday went around the school telling other students he had hooked up with Kelly that night and was telling some nasty lies. The boy did not know she was Dana's sister. Dana was on his way to beat this boy to a bloody pulp for lying about his sister. After hearing his story, I couldn't tell him not to do it — a beating seemed justified to me.

Later I found out half the students in the school were on their way to the store to watch the confrontation. When Dana arrived at the store and confronted the boy about what he said about his sister, the boy denied all of it. Dana became enraged because the boy lied to him. Dana got loud and started swearing and calling the boy outside, telling him, he was going to kick his ass for what he had done. All the customers were now looking, trying to see what was going on. The store manager threw Dana and all his friends out of the store and threatened to call the police. Dana left, but after that, all the boys at school steered clear of his sister; and if some boy did try to meet her, the minute they found out she was Dana's sister, they never came around again.

During Dana's high school years, our house was the house all his friends came to when getting ready to go out for the night on a weekend. I would walk down the hallway past the main bathroom, which was a large room, and all the boys would be primping and posing, flexing their arms and fixing their hair ten different ways, in front of the mirror. There was so much cologne splashing around it smelled like a French whorehouse.

Our house was also the house they came back to at night to sleep if they had too much to drink. My rule regarding drinking for Dana and his sister was that they could drink (I knew they would anyway) but wherever they were that was where they stayed. They were never, ever to get into a car with anyone who had been drinking. We had many overnight guests on the weekends. If I wasn't working on Sunday morning, I would get up and face a stereo speaker down the hallway where the bedrooms were. I'd place a tape of Irish music in the stereo and turn the volume up full blast. I would then watch as bedroom doors opened and heads popped out to see how many guests I had from Saturday night. I would then inform them all they had thirty minutes to get ready and be in my car, that we were going to church and I was not walking into church late. I didn't like the priest at the church we attended, who, if you walked in late, always made an issue of it by stopping what he was doing or he included your late entrance in a comment in his sermon. I would get all kinds of excuses from Dana's friends as to why they didn't need to go to church with me — like they went Saturday night or they were going home and would go with their family — unfortunately for them that didn't fly with me. If they were in my house on Sunday morning, then they were going to church with me.

One Sunday I had a whole pew full with me: Dana, Kelly, and four boys who had spent the night. The smell of booze coming from the boys' breath was overwhelming, I was passing out gum and mints through the whole mass. I worked many Sunday mornings because I was on call for the recovery room, and our hospital had the trauma helicopter for a large area covering four states so I would get called in a lot on the weekends. For the boys so inclined to drink too much, spending Saturday night at my house was like playing Russian roulette: maybe they would have to go to church with me and maybe they would be spared because of my work schedule. I suppose it beat going home the night before drunk and facing their parents.

Dana has a big sweet tooth, and when we first moved to Vegas, on Sundays we would go to the Show Boat on Boulder Highway after church. We would bowl a couple strings and have breakfast. Dana always ordered the same thing for breakfast: a waffle that was buried in strawberries and whipped cream. He is also very fond of the giant chocolate peanut-butter cups. They sell them at Sanborns candy store at Hampton Beach.

When Dana was struggling to get the UFC up and running, I decided to send him a box of the giant chocolate peanut-butter cups from Sanborn's Candies. Whenever Dana was at the beach, he would always go to Sanborn's and buy the giant peanut-butter cups. I thought it would lift his spirits a little; it's always nice when you get a little something from someone and it's not a special occasion. It was summer time, and in Las Vegas that means temperatures of anywhere from 105 degrees to 118 degrees. I never thought about the temperature out there when I sent him the chocolates. I hadn't heard from Dana and after about a week, I called and asked him if he received the package I sent. He told me he had gotten it, but he didn't say anything else so I asked him how they were. He said, "Mom, it's 110 degrees out here. How do you think they were?" It was not connecting at all for me, and then he said, "They were totally melted into one big nasty mess." So much for my well-intentioned surprise.

Only once did I have to pick up Dana and his sister at juvenile hall. They had been arrested together. Dana's sister was spending the night at a friend's house and had told me that her friend's mom would be home all weekend. Kelly had never lied to me, so I didn't call her friend's mom to verify that she would be home. The mother was not home but in California for the weekend. Kelly's friend thought it would be a good time to have a party. The party was crashed by a gang of kids that Kelly and her friend didn't know. They started trashing the house and wouldn't leave. Kelly's friend called the police to break up the party, but Kelly and her friend had been drinking and both were drunk. Dana had heard there was a party at this address and just happened to pull up to the house as the police were taking his sister out of the house in handcuffs. He decided he would rescue her. Dana charged the police, knocking them to the ground, grabbed his sister, threw her over his shoulder, and started running toward his car with her. He obviously did not get far with her before the police grabbed them both. One of the police officers kept asking Dana what kind of a moron would try to grab somebody the police were arresting and run from them. He asked him if he was mentally slow.

At four o'clock in the morning, I receive a call that both my kids have been arrested and were locked up in juvenile hall. At first I thought the phone call was someone playing a practical joke because, when Kelly and her friend were leaving my house, her friend turned to me and said, "You can come get us out of jail later tonight." I told her that wasn't funny. When this female voice told me both my children were in jail, I started to get mad, thinking it was the girls playing a joke. It only took a minute to realize that was not the case and they really were in jail.

When I picked them up, Dana told me how they both ended up being arrested. I honestly could not be mad at Dana for his attempt to rescue his sister, no matter how misguided, and it all ended well anyway. The father of Kelly's friend was an important politician, and when I went to pick up Dana and Kelly, I told the people at juvenile hall I would take Kelly's friend home with us also. They refused to release her to me and stated that, if her parents couldn't be bothered to stay home and take care of her, she could just stay in jail until one of them could be bothered to come and get her. Kelly's friend was screaming from her cell, "You just wait until my dad finds out about this. You'll all be looking for another job." The next morning she was brought to court in shackles with a number of other, mostly male, inmates. Her father arrived from his ranch in northern Nevada just in time to see his daughter dragged into court. Heads were rolling soon after he arrived and the court went into an immediate recess. All the charges were dropped against Dana, Kelly, and her friend who had the party.

Our door was always open to Dana and Kelly's friends while they we lived in Las Vegas. For example, one of Dana's friends was having a ration of problems at home. His mother and father were divorced and his mother had remarried. Dana, this friend, and one other boy who hung around with Dana all through high school were arrested together one day. The friend with problems at home had taken Dana and the other boy with him one night to get some money at his mother's house before the boys went out for the night. The mother and stepfather claimed their son stole the money from them and called the police. The following day they had all three boys arrested on some very serious charges. I could not believe it when Dana and his friends told me their side of the story. I called the boy's parents to explain what the boys had told me. I couldn't believe what assholes this boy's parents were. They refused to drop the charges against any of the boys and said this would teach them a good lesson. I tried to tell them this was overkill and it would do more than teach them a lesson, it would ruin their lives. These people couldn't have cared less about the consequences this would have for all three boys, including their son. I was appalled and totally pissed off.

I went to the District Attorney's office and told them I wanted Dana's case separated from the other two boys' cases. The first person I spoke with said that was not going to happen and just would not budge on the issue or reduce the charges. However, the day the boys were to appear in court I went to the courthouse early, I spoke with one of the attorneys from the prosecutor's office and worked out a deal to separate Dana's case from the other two boys' cases. I also got them to throw out most of the charges once I explained what had really happened. The final charge was changed to a misdemeanor. When the third boy's mother found out I had worked out this deal for Dana, she threw a fit and eventually got the same deal for her son.

The prosecutor who originally refused to separate the cases was not happy when he found out I had worked out a deal. There was little anyone could do at that point because Dana's case had already gone before the judge and been decided. I was not mad at Dana for that one either. I believed the three boys when they told me they did not steal any money. The boy whose house they had gone to said his parents always left money in the house and he took some whenever he needed it. The boy ran away from home a couple of times, and he would end up at our house. His father found out the boy was staying with us, and he called one night to say he would have me arrested if his son spent one more night in my house. I felt terrible, but I had to tell the young man that he had to go home. Eventually he turned to drugs in a big way, and later he committed suicide.

Our home in Las Vegas looked like a small cottage from the front. It was a one-story house, and when you first came in the double front door, there was an entry with a built-in bench. If you turned right, you went into the living room, and turning left brought you into a short hallway that led to the kitchen and then through the dining room and into the TV room at the back of the house. At the back of that room were sliding glass doors that led to the back yard.

One evening, I was sitting in the back room watching television, and out of the corner of my eye, I noticed something run across the floor. I was not sure what it was, but I HATE spiders and there are lots of spiders in Las Vegas, and some very big ones. I was worried it was some enormous arachnid in the room with me, and I could not watch the television anymore. I was too worried about what I saw and where it had gone. There were long drapes by the sliding glass doors, and I saw something start to climb up the edge of one of them. I was very relieved to see it was not a huge spider but a tiny field mouse. The mouse climbed about two and a half feet up the curtain and then stopped and was staring over at me. It was the cutest little thing, and I decided I did not mind this little creature being in the house as long as he did not venture into the kitchen. Quite often, he would climb up the curtain, sit there, and watch me or whoever was watching television. The mouse never appeared in any other rooms in the house. He was like a little guest who would sit with you while you watched television. Unfortunately, baby mice began to appear in the television room after a few months and soon there were a number of little mice running around. I was told that, if I did not do something, before I knew it the house would be full of mice. Reluctantly, I went looking for something that I thought would be a humane way of getting rid of my little friend and his many offspring. I did not want to kill him, just move him out of the house.

I found a product that said it was humane and that trapped mice did not suffer. It was a small box, approximately four inches by four inches and a half-inch deep that held a clear gel on the bottom of it. The theory was that, when the mouse walked across the gel, it would get stuck, and you could remove the creature from the house. That is exactly what happened — our little friend was stuck in the gel — but removing it from the house did not include getting the mouse out of the gel. Eventually, it would die of hunger or dehydration — hardly humane.

Dana was in high school at this time, and he came home to find the little mouse struggling to get out of the gel. Dana took the box and the mouse it held out on the sidewalk in front of the house. He thought he was going to be able to lift the little creature out of the gel and set him free. After three or four minutes, Dana came back in, upset that he could not get the mouse's feet free from the gel. I told him to get a spoon and just lift the gel where the mouse's feet were. He said he needed me help him. As I headed outside with Dana, I grabbed a spoon from the kitchen.

We sat on the sidewalk, and I held the box while Dana tried to scoop the gel out from under the little guy's feet, but the gel did not budge. It was really quite traumatizing for the mouse and for Dana. The mouse was actually making little noises that sounded like it was crying. It was horrible. We tried for five minutes to free him, but we could not. Then the worst thing happened. While trying to get one of his feet loose, the mouse fell over and now the whole side of his little body was stuck to the gel. I couldn't take any more and told Dana I was going back into the house. There was nothing more we could do. Dana didn't leave the mouse for another ten minutes, but then he came back into the house very upset over what had just happened to our little house guest. We moved the box up under some bushes where we figured the mouse would be out of sight of cats and would just die. Dana remained distraught over what had happened and so did I.

I cannot figure out how someone who was so caring and compassionate about this little mouse's fate changed so deeply and profoundly. Dana recently told me he had bought a bulldog puppy, and that he came home one night to find the dog had done something that absolutely infuriated him. Dana did not say what the dog had done, but he said he chased that dog around the house and the yard for ten minutes and beat the hell out of it, and then he got rid of it. How do you go from someone who was traumatized by the pain of a little field mouse to someone who thinks it is appropriate to chase down and beat a puppy? What happened over those years to create such an angry, hostile man?

As I said previously, Las Vegas has lots of little critters, like scorpions, black widow and brown recluse spiders, and huge cockroaches — the locals call them water bugs but they are huge cockroaches. Every month I had an exterminator spray the house inside and out and the block wall that enclosed the side and back yards. I had discovered that the black widows like to make nests in the cinderblocks in the block walls, and so I made sure the exterminator sprayed the wall heavily.

While in high school in Las Vegas, Dana had a problem with his big toenail growing into the side of his toe, which would then cause an infection and bleeding and was extremely painful. On three different occasions, I had to bring him to the doctor to have the toenail removed. Each time, they cut the toenail out from the top of the nail all the way to the bottom, under the skin and halfway across the toe, and then put an application of acid on the area to try to prevent the nail from growing back into the side of the toe. We were at home after one of the nail removals, and Dana's girlfriend at the time was visiting. Dana had just come out of the shower and had on a bathrobe and a pair of my green operating room scrubs. His girlfriend was sitting at the dining room table and I was in the kitchen (the kitchen was open to the dining room) when Dana walked over, pulled out one of the chairs at the dining room table, and sat down. He lifted his leg with the bad toe and placed it on the chair next to the one his girlfriend was sitting in. Her mouth opened and she had this awful look on her face as she pointed to Dana's foot. She had not seen Dana's foot since they had removed most of his toenail, and so Dana thought she was horrified by its appearance. For what seemed like an entire minute, she just kept pointing at his foot. Not a word came out of her mouth. Dana finally leaned forward and looked down at what she was pointing at.

I didn't know at that point what he had seen, but like a rocket, Dana came up out of the chair, tearing off the bathrobe and jumping around the dining room. He was kicking his leg in the air and jumping around the room like an Irish step dancer as he tried to untie the waist belt of the O.R. scrubs he was wearing. I was laughing so hard I could hardly move until his girlfriend told me it was a black widow walking up his pant leg. I began screaming at Dana to run outside and not knock the spider off in the house, but by that point, he was already kicking the pants off his leg and high into the air. The pants landed on the floor in the dining room, and I ran over to see if the spider was still on the pants. It was not. It was now loose in the house somewhere. We searched for ten minutes and could not find the black widow anywhere. I did find it a week later. The spider was huge and had built a web between the refrigerator and the kitchen cabinets. I killed it. I can honestly say the dancers in "The Lord of the Dance" do not jump or kick as high as Dana did when he saw that spider on his pants.

About this time, I thought Dana was becoming inconsiderate of others and taking on an air about himself that I did not care for. We were middle class working people just like most other people. Although we perhaps had a little more than a lot of others, that was only because I worked eighty to a hundred hours a week to afford it.

I used to take vacation time on occasion to travel to Mexico with medical teams out of Texas and Las Vegas to do surgery on mostly children with cleft lips and cleft palates. The Indians in the mountains had no access to medical care, and they had a very high incidence of cleft lip and cleft palate. People in the villages shunned many of these children because of their appearance. Some of these children were horribly disfigured, but the surgery made them look very normal and was life changing for them and their families. It was also life changing for us, the people doing the operations. It was very humbling to see how little these people had and yet they were happy, friendly, and so appreciative for any little thing we could do for them. Sometimes the mothers and fathers would walk for days with their child when they heard the American doctors were coming.

I cleared bringing Dana along on one of these trips, thinking that seeing how fortunate he really was compared to millions of people in this world might change him. Much to my surprise, however, Dana wanted no part of it and absolutely refused to go. His sister, who was fifteen at the time, went on a short three-day trip with us instead, and it had a huge influence on her. I really wish Dana had gone. It may have been an experience that would have made a difference in the person he is today.

BOSTON

In 1988, I decided to move back east. In April of that year, I took a job with traveling nurses and headed to Martha's Vineyard to work in their hospital for the summer. After the summer job, I was going to head to New York City to live. I love New York City and think it is the best city in the world. I thought it would be helpful to have a second driver and not drive alone across country, and so I made Dana accompany me. For all the help he was, however, I should have just driven by myself.

When we reached the east coast, I decided to stop in New York City for a few days. When living in Las Vegas, I would fly to New York just before Christmas and spend a week there, shopping, going to shows, and going out to dinner. We tended to frequent the same few of bars every year, and I would see many of the same people each time I returned. One bar we spent a good amount of time in was P.J. Carneys on Seventh Avenue up by 58th near the Park. We became friendly with the owners, the people who worked there, and some of the regulars. Carneys was a small place, but during the holidays when we were there, it was always packed and we had a good time. One of the regulars I had met at Carneys was an opera singer. He had a most gorgeous voice and was obviously and openly gay. When Dana and I first went to Carneys, my gay friend immediately came over and wanted to know who Dana was. The people I had come to know at Carneys had met Dana's sister on a couple of previous trips to New York, but Dana had never accompanied me. The place was full, and my friend was quite drunk, telling us it was his birthday and all he wanted for his birthday was Dana. Dana immediately wanted to know who he was and how I knew him. The second night in New York we went back up to Carneys and as we walked in my friend came running over to us, grabbed Dana and gave him a kiss, and as quickly as he had come over to us, flittered off talking to someone else. That was typical of him I thought nothing of it and no one else who knew him did either. I headed to an empty seat at the bar, and Dana walked past me and went straight into the men's room. He was in there forever, and when he came out, I said, "Are you okay? You were in the bathroom for ten minutes."

He said, "I can't believe your friend just kissed me in front of everyone in this bar. I think I'm going to throw up."

I said, "Are you kidding? Did you even see anyone look when he did it? No one cares. That's just him, and he's probably kissed half the guys in here at one time or another." Dana was horrified and could not get over it.

The housing at the Vineyard did not work out, and I was staying in someone's basement bedroom. One of the nurses I was working with told me she was going up to Boston on weekends to work for nursing temp agencies and making good money. On one of my days off, I headed up to Boston and interviewed with a couple of temp agencies. I decided I was going to leave the Vineyard and move up to Boston for the summer. I found a great furnished one-bedroom apartment that was a fifth floor walkup in the North End on Salem Street.

Dana had flown back to Vegas and was living with his father, who had moved out to Las Vegas after we did — so much for getting away from him. Dana called one night and was whispering into the phone because he didn't want his father to hear him. The two of them were not getting along at all, and Dana asked if I could buy him a plane ticket to come to Boston. He said he could not take another day living with his dad. His father heard him on the phone and picked up the phone and began screaming and swearing that Dana was not working, slept half the day away, and then went out all night with his friends. His father said he was ready to kick him out of his house. I bought Dana a ticket to come back to Boston before his dad killed him.

Dana arrived at night, and had a cab bring him to the apartment because I was at work. The North End in Boston has very narrow streets with buildings one on top of the other, and most of the buildings are brick and four to six stories high. The buildings are very old and very charming — old world charm is what I would call it. The North End is a world apart from Vegas, which is all new construction and strip malls on every corner. There are no high rises. Vegas was what Dana was used to, and when the cabbie started driving down Salem Street, Dana told him, "Buddy, you're in the wrong neighborhood. My mom would never live here."

The cabbie pulled up to the address Dana had given him and said, "This is it, pal. Get out."

I was working 7 p.m. to 7 a.m., and so I didn't see Dana until the next morning. When I got home, he told me he could not believe I was living in this place. The apartment was a one bedroom, fifth-floor walkup. The street level of the building was a butcher shop, and during the day, they would have rabbits hanging out front, tied by their feet to the metal awning pole. There was always an entire row of them to greet you at the front door of the building. We had a big beautiful house in Las Vegas, a little over twenty-nine hundred square feet with five bedrooms, two bathrooms, living room, TV room, dining room, den, and a pool in the backyard. This one bedroom fifth-floor walkup was very different from what Dana was used to. I loved it. Dana would eventually too.

After a few days, I told Dana he needed to get out and look for a job. He was not going to lie around the apartment all day. I was working seven days a week for a nursing temp agency at Brigham and Women's Hospital. After a week of coming home every morning and finding Dana in my bed sleeping, I gave him an ultimatum: "Get your ass up and find a job or get out." He was nineteen years old and needed to start being a little more responsible. When I got home the next morning, he was up and out; but then I found a note saying he had gone to Maine.

Dana returned from Maine a short time later with his girlfriend, Brenda, whom he had apparently been dating his senior year in Maine. In his absence, I had moved from the Salem Street apartment to a larger one-bedroom apartment on Tileston Street. Dana and Brenda had now both moved in with me. They were sleeping on the living room floor on a stack of comforters. Brenda found a job right away at one of the department stores at Downtown Crossing, and eventually Dana got a job working at the Black Rose, a great Irish bar next to Faneuil Hall off State Street. The bar is still there today, unlike so many other places that have long since disappeared. Dana, who was a doorman and bouncer, did not work there for very long; it seems he was in more fights than he prevented. The employees at the Black Rose were Dana's age and Irish, right off the boat. The Irish are a lot of fun and have a great outlook on life in general, and Dana got along with them really well. Dana and Brenda eventually moved to South Boston and shared an apartment with four of the Irish guys he was working with.

When we lived on Tileston Street, I would get up in the morning to go to work to find the crust of two loaves of bread and all the crumbs on the kitchen counter — every morning. The loaves were broken in half and all hollowed out in the center. When Dana worked at the Black Rose, he did not get home until around three or four in the morning. His path home always took him down Salem Street to Tileston Street. Bova's Bakery is on the corner of Salem and Prince Streets; open seven days a week, three hundred sixty-five days a year. All you can smell at that hour is the aroma of fresh bread and pastries baking especially in the winter when it is freezing out. When it is cold, it seems like the smell of the bread baking lingers in the air and the warmth of the glow of lights from inside calls out to you to come inside. Dana could never pass by without going in and buying a couple loaves of fresh bread right out of the oven. He didn't like the crust, so he would break it open and dig out all the warm, soft bread inside. The remnants were what were on the kitchen counter every morning.

Dana worked nights and Brenda worked days, and so they did not get to see much of each other. One afternoon, Dana decided to meet Brenda on her lunch break and have lunch with her. Brenda was running late, and Dana was standing out in front of Woolworths on Washington Street at downtown crossing waiting for her. It was a winter day and bitterly cold out. As Dana leaned up against the building, watching people as they walked by, a businessman in his early thirties was walking down the street with his hands in the pockets of his overcoat. Three black men who were standing near Dana ran up behind the businessman and hit him in the back of the head so forcefully that it sent him flying down onto the sidewalk. The man they attacked didn't even have time to pull his hands out of his pockets to break his fall; he never knew what hit him.

As the man lay face down on the ground unconscious, his attackers began to rifle through his pockets, robbing him. Other people on the street continued to walk by, ignoring the whole scene as if nothing was going on. Dana ran over and confronted the men who were robbing the unconscious man, the three of them turned on Dana and started calling him white pudding and telling him he better back off before he got the same thing. Dana had just begun to fight with the three of them when police sirens were heard coming down the street. The three men took off running. Dana bent over the man, who was still unconscious on the sidewalk, trying to see what he could do to help him when the police pulled up, jumped out, and grabbed Dana. Just as no one stopped to help the man who was attacked, no one was coming forward to help Dana now. Finally, one woman told the police it was not Dana who had attacked the man, that he was the only person who tried to help him. The police let Dana go. Dana never did meet Brenda for lunch, and when he got back to the apartment, he was so hyped up on adrenaline that it took him twenty minutes to calm down. He was mad that not one single person — and downtown crossing is packed with people at that time of day — stopped to help this man. He also blamed poor Brenda for his getting involved in the incident because she was not out of work on time to meet him for lunch.

Dana would have a number of jobs while living in Boston. One summer he worked construction with his best friend at the time, an Irish kid name Richie McDonough. They worked laying blacktop and paving in the heat of the summer. Dana says that was the worst job he ever had and that it gave him a very good sense of what he did not want to do for a living.

Richie eventually moved back to Ireland and opened his own bar in Limerick. Soon after Richie moved back to Ireland, Dana decided it would be fun to go to Ireland and surprise Richie over the holidays. Dana, Brenda, and I booked a flight to arrive after Christmas, and we planned to stay until after New Years. I had been to Ireland with friends on three different occasions, and so I knew what to expect. Mrs. Walsh, was a woman who ran a B&B and with whom we always stayed when we flew into Shannon Airport. We arranged to stay with her for the week. Mrs. Walsh loved Dana. She would do his laundry for him and would sit and talk with him, always offering to fix him something to eat or drink. It was quite the surprise for Richie when we came walking into his pub. One thing I have learned about the Irish is that the holidays are one big drinking fest. Dana, Brenda, and I actually went out during the day to do some sightseeing, but if we stopped at the pub first, that was the end of anything except drinking all day and all night. We met a couple of Scotsmen who came into Richie's pub. They had come to Ireland on holiday and, six months later, were still there. The two of them were absolute mad men. They had bought the cutest little pub out in the country and we all went there one night. What a night that was. I remember Richie pulling a bunch of Christmas lights off the walls and, with the lights still lit, wrapping them around himself, and then jumping up on a table and standing there like a giant Christmas tree, singing, hollering, and drinking his beer. I am surprised he wasn't electrocuted.

Dana had a pair of green plaid flannel pants that pulled on and tied at the waist. He wore them a couple of times when we went to Richie's pub. All the Irish guys would be all over him about those pants, taking the piss out of him for going out in public wearing them. Dana said he thought he was going to die before we ever left Ireland. He didn't like the food, which was mostly fried, and he never had so much to drink in all his life.

One of our first days in Ireland, we set out to do some sightseeing and pulled over to the side of the road to take some video of a group of caravans that were set up off the road. We were barely there a minute when three men charged at the car. Dana saw them coming and barely got the window rolled up and the door locked before they reached us demanding we give them the video camera. They were hollering at Dana, "Why are you taking pictures of us." Dana kept trying to tell them we were just tourists taking pictures, but they didn't want to hear that. Their tone and demeanor were escalating by the minute and they were getting louder and more threatening. Dana put the car in gear and peeled out. After telling Richie what had happened, we discovered later they were gypsies and he told us we were lucky to have gotten out of there. He said the gypsies do not like anyone taking pictures of them. We were clueless as to what gypsies even were. It was a great trip and a lot of fun, but it is hard not to have a good time in Ireland.

Dana worked as a night butler and bellman at the Boston Harbor Hotel from 1990 to 1992, followed by jobs at the Westin and the Four Seasons. Now when Dana is in Boston, he stays in the suites at these hotels, which is more than a touch ironic. While working at the Boston Harbor Hotel, Dana met quite the cast of characters. A couple of them were true Southie boys. They were charming, witty, and good looking in their own way, and when they got together, oh the stories they would tell. The amazing part is that the stories were all true. They didn't need to embellish them at all. Dana loved hanging with these guys. A number of Southie boys would be in Dana's wedding, and John Barry, (Baso) would be his best man.

There was a story one of them told me about someone owing his friend money, and the person who owed the money had decided he was not going to pay the money back. One night, they paid a visit to the person who owed the money. They kicked open his door and stuck a gun in the man's mouth and told him that he either paid back the money in a week or else. It was a simple enough story, but before all of this happened a friend had told me, they thought the person with the gun looked like Howdy Doodie. When I heard the story, I dubbed him the Howdy Doodie killer, though I did not tell him that. Never judge a book by its cover.

For a brief period, I had a business in the Financial District in downtown Boston, a concierge service serving some of the high-rise office buildings. Dana came to me at work one day and said, "Mom, I need six hundred dollars, and I need it today." He had no job at the time, and I assumed the money was probably for his rent, but I asked him why he needed this money so urgently. He informed me he owed a bookie who had given him to the end of the day to pay up. Dana apparently had put a bet on a game and lost.

I asked him, "How could you bet six hundred dollars you don't have and that you know you're not going to have because you have no job."

He told me it was a sure thing! Obviously not. I gave him the money because I didn't want to see him in the hospital for the next month, but he had to work it off. I was not just going to let him pay me back when he got a job. Dana worked for me for two weeks as a bike courier in downtown Boston in the middle of winter to pay off the money I gave him.

Although Boston is a big city, it still has the feeling of a small town. At one time, both my kids were living in Boston, and Boston holds lots of good memories of good times and good friends for all of us. Dana's sister was going to college there and lived in the dorm, and she would move back in with me during summer breaks. By then I had a much larger two-bedroom apartment. She worked while going to college, as a waitress for a while and then was hired to work in the emergency room at Brigham and Women's Hospital, where I worked. So many days we worked together and there were times I would walk into a bar to find one or both of my kids there.

One bar we would go to frequently, was Pete's on Broad Street in downtown Boston, our version of Cheer's. Dana called one night around ten o'clock and said, "Mom, I'm at Pete's with Kenny. Come down and have a beer with us." Kenny was Dana's cousin from Maine. I had just recently moved to an apartment in Southie from the North End, and I told him I would be down in about twenty minutes.

Pete's was a small bar, long and narrow with old, red brick walls, a few tables against the side wall, with a great juke box, and two more small tables at the very back of the bar. There was just enough space between the barstools and the tables for one person to walk by. When I arrived at Pete's, Dana and Kenny were sitting at the bar. The place was crowded, as usual, and I joined them at the bar for a beer. Dana had been there for a few hours, and he obviously had quite a few beers, and was in good form. Around midnight, Kelly, Dana's sister came walking into Pete's with two security guards who worked at Brigham and Women's Hospital. They had all just gotten out of work. The three of them headed back to the tables at the back of the bar. After they ordered drinks, I saw this guy go back and start talking to Kelly. I'm not sure why he picked her out because the two security guards with her were big guys, body builders.

I could hear this person talking to Kelly, and he was being a real jackass. After a few minutes of watching him, I told Dana, "We need to pay our tab and leave, and I need you to go get your sister to leave with us." Dana asked me why, and I told him that some guy would not leave her alone. We all got up and left together, but this person followed us out and started up again. I turned to him and told him to go back inside and leave us alone.

He says, "Shut the fuck up, you bitch."

He never saw what was coming at him. Before he got the word "bitch" out, Dana punched him in the face, breaking his nose. We began walking away and out of nowhere, six guys jumped on Dana in the middle of Broad Street. The two security guards, who were just getting in their car, saw these people jump Dana and came running back to pull the pile of people off him. A couple more guys jumped on them, and the next thing you know, it looked like a scene out of some movie. Cars were stopped on State Street as bodies were falling on the street in front of them and rolling over the hoods of the cars. As the fight moved down State Street across from the Black Rose, Kelly was trying to pull away one of the guys who was kicking Dana, who was now lying on the road, off of him. One of them turned towards Kelly and punched her in the face, sending her flying onto the pavement.

At that moment, a group of six or seven people visiting from Chicago came walking out of the Black Rose and saw Kelly get hit.

They ran over to defend her, and by the time the police arrived with three or four cruisers and a paddy wagon, there had to be twenty guys fighting over a city block area.

When it was all over, we couldn't find Dana. We were afraid that someone had pulled a knife and that he was hurt somewhere. The last time we saw him, he was lying in the street with guys kicking him in the head and back and stomach. We spent an hour looking for him, and then we went home and started calling hospital emergency rooms. Finally, he called us — he was fine. When the police came, he ran into one of the parking garages and hid.

The person with the broken nose was arrested, and later he tried to sue Dana for assault. Dana had NO money back then. Apparently starting fights was something this person and his friends did often, but I'm sure he never ended up with a broken nose before.

Dana did not do the brightest things when he was drinking, which is why he quit, and he always had a short fuse so it didn't really take a lot to set him off if he'd had a few beers. He was at Hampton Beach one night with one of his uncles when he got in a fight at one of the bars. They both were thrown out of the bar. I'm not sure what happened from that point on, but the police called his girlfriend the next day and told her they had Dana's wallet. Someone found it and the police officer said he could come down to the station to pick it up. I then get a call from Dana, who told me he was not sure where his truck was, but he thought he drove it into the marsh the night before and —oh by the way — he may have killed a person in a fight. I thought I was going to throw up when he told me that. Worse yet, he said he had a hatchet in his truck and he may have hit the person with it. I was nauseous with that one.

I told him that the police had called his girlfriend to inform her that they had his wallet. I told him, "Find your truck and get home, and do not go to the police station for your wallet until I can find out what really happened."

I spent the rest of the day making calls to see if there was anyone killed in a fight. I finally was able to get hold of my brother who had no idea what Dana was talking about. He told me they were thrown out of a bar after getting into a fight and Dana had driven his truck into the marsh. He said he didn't know why Dana's truck wound up in the marsh, but he said that was the extent of what happened the previous night. Dana must have dreamed he got in the second fight and killed the person. Thank God, it didn't really happen.

Dana was in trouble again one night when he and Brenda had dinner at a sports bar near their apartment in Weymouth. As they were leaving, some idiot thought it would be amusing to grab Brenda's ass on the way out the door. Dana chased him down in the parking lot and confronted him. The guy admitted he did it and thought it was funny. He didn't think it was funny for very long because Dana punched him in the face and broke his jaw. The police were called and Dana was arrested. The judge ordered Dana to pay all this persons hospital bills, but Dana had no money and eventually they attached his paycheck to pay the bills. It cost Dana good money, but I am sure that person will forever think twice about grabbing someone's girlfriend.

Dana and Brenda lived together for a number of years, and one day Dana just decided he did not want to live with anyone, that he wanted to be by himself, or so he said. Dana and Brenda had been making plans to move to Atlanta so this all seemed to come out of nowhere. Brenda didn't really have a life of her own. She had no friends outside of work because she was always with Dana, which was how he wanted it. Dana did not let her know that things were over. Brenda came home from work one day to an empty apartment, and I do mean empty. Dana had not only moved out but also taken all the furniture, and their rent was due the next week and Brenda didn't have enough money to pay it. Dana just told her to go back to Maine.

Brenda was a petite, quiet, girl, but she was not about to let Dana send her packing back to Maine because he had decided he did not want to be with her anymore. When Dana found out Brenda was not moving back to Maine, he went around telling all his friends he would kill the first one who asked her out — he knew they all wanted to. Boston has an abundance of good looking men, and Brenda is a beautiful, exotic looking girl. Every guy that met

Brenda wanted to go out with her. In fact, she dated Nomar Garcia Para when he played for the Red Sox.

Dana's sister and I were furious with Dana when we found out what he had done to Brenda. She had no furniture, no money to pay the rent, and nowhere to go. I can't imagine coming home from work to find an empty apartment, knowing my rent is due and I have no money to pay it. I called Brenda and asked her what she was going to do. She told me she didn't know, but she was not moving back to Maine and she had to be out of the apartment in a few days because she didn't have enough money to pay rent. I told her she could move in with me until she could get things together and find her own place. I'm sure that was just what she wanted to do, move in with her ex-boyfriends mother, but I was never home and I had an extra bedroom, so it was not as if we would even see each other that much. Reluctantly, she said okay and moved in.

Brenda and I had become friends when she and Dana were living with me on Tileston Street in the North End, so I knew she was someone I could live with without any problems. I cannot say that about very many people. When Dana and Brenda lived with me, I dragged Brenda out with me a few nights to the bars. Dana would be furious with both of us. We went into the Black Rose at the end of one night of drinking, and Dana was on the door. Dana told us both to go home, that we were not going in, but we just laughed and walked right past him. Once inside, Dana told the other people he worked with to keep everyone away from his girlfriend and his mom. They actually threw one person out who bought us drinks and was talking to us. The poor guy couldn't figure out why he had been asked to leave. I found it quite funny, but Dana was livid with both of us. He had no sense of humor, even back then.

Brenda and I are still friends today. She married a firefighter named Dave (Dana's loss), and his parents own a beach house right around the corner from mine at Hampton Beach in New Hampshire.

Before his venture into MMA, Dana was a huge fan of boxing, but these days he's right boxing is a dying sport, your fathers or even grandfather's sport. One year while we were all living in Boston, I went out to the Brimfield Fair, and while rummaging through all the vendors items I came across a half dozen really great, old newspaper articles about old time boxers, boxing matches, and an old magazine featuring a boxer on the cover. I bought them and took them to an art store and had them all matted and framed. I then placed them in a large box that had once contained a floor lamp, one of those cheap, ugly black floor lamps. Dana came to my apartment Christmas morning, and sees this big box with his name on it under the tree. I could tell he had no clue what it could be. He always liked to guess what was in the boxes, and he was usually good at it, but not this time. So not being able to figure out what it was he couldn't wait to open the present. He ripped open the wrapping paper, excited about what it was he had gotten, and then he saw the picture on the side of the box that showed the ugly floor lamp. The look on his face changed in a hurry. It went from excitement to disappointment. Dana looked at me and said, "What the hell is this?"

I told him, "I thought you needed a lamp in the living room in your apartment. Don't you want it?"

He realized he was being a bit of a jerk and said, "Oh no, this is fine." The look on his face had not changed. I told him to open the box and see how the lamp looked, and I said that the lamp needed to be put together. Begrudgingly, he opened the box, and at first he looked a little confused. Then he pulled out one of the framed pictures. Now the look on his face changed once again, he was so excited when he realized what it was: first, that his gift was about boxing, and second, that it was not a floor lamp for his apartment. After that, Dana looked for boxing pictures and magazines wherever he went, and so did I. Dana has developed quite a collection now. Ali is Dana's favorite fighter and a few years ago, Lorenzo gave Dana four unbelievably beautiful, framed pictures of Ali.

Dana became good friends with Peter Welch, another Southie boy and the boxing coach on the first season of *The Ultimate Fighter*. Peter was a boxer in Southie and had been a member of the Board of Directors of the McDonough Boxing Training Center at the courthouse building on East Broadway. The local Southie paper did an article on the gym and the work people had done to help save it: "The gym, which had been dilapidated and dangerously close to being shut down, was saved by generous local donations and a dedicated new board of directors. The board consisted of Joseph Gray, Director; Dan Long, President; Dana White, Vice President; Peter Welch, Treasurer; Tom Atado, Facility Coordinator; Tournament Coordinator, Derek Barnes, ; and Administrative Trainer, Jim Gifford, ." Dana was quoted in the local Southie newspaper in an article on the gym: "Any youth that comes through that door and is willing to apply himself will get the best training in Massachusetts. In amateur boxing it is rare to get individual and specialized training, due to the fact that there is no money involved" (*The Southie News*, September 1994).

Peter and Dana began working together, and they set up a workout program called boxing aerobics. They were teaching it in most of the gyms and health clubs in Boston. Dana would later teach these classes in the gyms in Las Vegas when he moved back out there. Dana boxed training with Peter for a brief time, but he was hurt sparring one day and decided he would rather manage and train other people to box, than to be the one in the ring fighting.

Dana worked with Peter at the Pals gym, teaching and training young Southie kids to box. He was also teaching classes at the health clubs and gyms Peter had lined up. The classes were very popular at all the gyms, and Peter and Dana were very busy. Peter and Dana were like brothers, until one day, there was a huge falling out. Dana decided he had to leave Boston and get far away, and so he packed up and moved back to Vegas. I was very upset about Dana leaving because the fight was over a disagreement about money, but once again, this was a twist of fate for my son. Had Dana and Peter not had this falling out, there would be no UFC today because Dana would never have left Boston.

Peter runs a gym in Southie these days, and he and Dana are friends again. I imagine that, when Dana thinks back to his years in Boston, he recalls them as some of the best of his life, spent with some of the best friends of his life. Dana truly did have the best bunch of friends, and they did not care about money or who you were or where you came from. They hung out because they all got on so well together and had such a good time. One day not long ago, Baso, (another good friend of Danas from Southie) told me he would give anything to have his old friend Dana back, the Dana who would come knocking on his door and say, "Dude, I'm starving and have no money." Baso would make a couple peanut butter sandwiches and the two of them would sit on the couch in his house watching cartoons and eating their sandwiches. Dana was piss poor the whole time he lived in Boston — in 1993 Dana made a whopping $10,136 and listed his job as a boxing trainer — but I believe those were some of his happiest days.

There have been many articles about Dana and his life growing up. You would think he had a tough, horrible life that he was left alone, growing up by himself in the mean streets of Southie and Las Vegas. When Dana moved to Southie he was twenty years old. I would say his life to that point had been better than most people's his age. Dana complains that his dad was never around or there for him when he was growing up, but he does not realize how lucky he was that his dad, who was an abusive drunk and cared only about himself, was not part of his life. Dana had four uncles, who were always around and spent time with him, and two of his uncles had sailboats and he would go out sailing with them. His grandmother lived with us so someone was always home when Dana and his sister came home from school. We went skiing in Utah, and Dana spent his summers back east and in upstate Maine, where he had his own horse to ride and lots of cousins his age and aunts and uncles to spend time with. Dana's uncle in Connecticut lived on a lake, and when Dana visited, they went swimming and fishing. We would always go to Hampton Beach for a couple weeks every summer, and his aunts, uncles, and grandmother would all come up and stay with us. In fact, I wish I had his life growing up.

RETURN TO VEGAS

When Dana returned to Las Vegas, he had no idea what he was going to do. He had no money and no prospects. Almost all his friends he had gone to Bishop Gorman High School with were still living in Las Vegas, however, and one of them was Anne Stella. Anne worked at a salon as a manicurist, doing people's nails and lived at home with her parents and sisters when Dana met her after returning to Las Vegas. They started dating and soon they were married, but from day one, theirs was a turbulent union, a union straight from hell.

Dana went to the Department of Motor Vehicles as soon as he arrived in Las Vegas to get his license switched from Massachusetts to Nevada, but he found out that Maine had something in the national registry that would prevent him from getting his license in Nevada until he cleared up the problem in Maine. Dana called and told me what was going on. I asked him if he had a parking ticket or driving violation he hadn't taken care of before he left Maine, and he told me no. He then proceeded to tell me that he was supposed to appear in court. He had gotten into a fight in a 7-11 parking lot where he and some other high school kids were hanging out, the police were called, and he was arrested. He had decided he was close to graduation and would be leaving Maine and so he just didn't go to court for the incident. Now there was a warrant out for his arrest for failure to appear in court. Dana was lucky that fact was not available to the DMV or he would have been arrested on the spot in Las Vegas.

I told Dana to call the police station in Maine and see what he needed to do to take care of the issue. Of course, it was not going to be anything that easy. They told Dana there was nothing that could be done unless he returned to Maine. When Dana told me he was going to have to go back to Maine to clear up the problem, I explained that, if he went back like they wanted, he would be arrested the minute he showed up. I told him there had to be some other way. I then called the prosecutor's office to see what we could do without Dana returning to Maine, but they were having no part of it and said he would have to return to Maine.

It is funny how things work out sometimes, and this seems another twist of fate. It was March. My apartment in Southie was on the first floor of a three-decker on East Broadway, the main parade route for the Saint Patrick's Day parade — my apartment was always full that day. People in Southie just leave their doors open and people come and go as the parade goes by. Many times you don't even know half the people in your apartment. This St. Patrick's Day, the parade was over and I had an apartment full of people. One of the people in my apartment was a good friend of my neighbors on the second floor, and it turns out he was an attorney. I mentioned the problem Dana was having in Las Vegas, and the attorney told me, "Oh, I have a good friend who works in the prosecutor's office up there. We went to school together."

A few days later, the attorney called to say he talked with his friend, and he told me that, Dana absolutely should not return to Maine until this was resolved because the authorities wanted him to go to jail for not appearing and leaving the state. He said that his friend had taken care of the charges, and Dana just needed to hire an attorney in Maine to appear in court for him and the charges would be dropped. Dana called one of his uncles in Maine, who gave him the name of a local attorney. Dana sent the attorney the money to appear in court for him, and just as my St. Patty's Day friend told me would happen, the charges were dropped. This situation could have gone badly for Dana except for my chance meeting on St. Patrick's Day.

Dana had made the decision not to work for someone else but instead wanted to start his own business. He would call to tell me all these great ideas he had for a business, and in fact, a lot of them were very good ideas. Follow-through to completion was not Dana' strong suit at the time. Dana was too scattered in his planning and actions. He would get to a certain point with a business idea, and then he would have an idea for something else and want to start something new and abandon the idea he was working on.

Dana called one day and asked if I would come out to Las Vegas and help him get a business started. He kept saying he just did not know where or how to get started. I was out of work at the time due to a car accident and was waiting to have cervical surgery on a couple of herniated discs, so I had the time and I flew out to Las Vegas to help him. We decided he could call his business Dana White Enterprises, which left things wide open for what he could eventually do under that business name and didn't restrict him to any specific business type.

Dana and I went to a Kinko's in a strip mall and had business cards made up along with letterhead and envelopes. Just a classic black on white business card and off white paper and envelops. Dana at the time was living with Annie (his wife) and her parents, and so his business address was their home address. Dana and I worked together on a business plan, and Dana decided he would start by offering boxing aerobics classes at gyms in Las Vegas as he had been doing in Boston. I remember him saying to me, "What if they don't like my proposal, and say 'no thanks, we're not interested'?"

I would always ask him, "If they turn you down, will you be any worse off for having tried? But if they like your proposal and say yes, will you be better off?" I needed him to see rejection might hurt his ego but nothing else would change. Dana approached all the gyms, and the Q Sports Club was interested in the idea of something new and different in an aerobics workout for their members. A couple other gyms were interested as well.

Dana's classes became so popular that the gym was often over-flowing with people trying to get into them. An article in the *Review Journal* dated August 16, 1996 reported, "Dana O'Del, aerobic director for Q The Sports Club, said that when White came to her over a year ago to begin a serious boxing class at the Q, class attendance was much smaller. 'We had 20 to 25 when we started a year ago; we have 70 to 75 now,' she said. 'It is the only class that has grown so much.' Private classes cost about $40, while five week clinics cost $125." Dana also set up a jump rope workout that was convenient for business people who traveled a lot. Dana told the *Review Journal*, "You get more benefit than you would from a Stairmaster or a treadmill. Jumping rope not only provides an intense cardiovascular workout; it actually burns almost as many calories as running. Over time, it greatly improves your coordination, and a rope can go anywhere with no hassle" (*Review Journal*, January 11, 1997). Many members of the Q were executives who needed the stress release of working out and wanted to be in shape to stay on top of their game, and many people in his classes wanted private lessons with Dana at their homes. Others were asking Dana to set up gyms in their homes or office buildings. The Fertitta's had Dana set up a gym in their executive office building to make it convenient for them and their executives to stay in shape. In those early days, Dana listened to motivational tapes all the time and felt they were very helpful in moving forward with his plans for his future.

A group of people who worked at Nevada Title Insurance Company were Dana's clients, and they were very helpful to Dana in the beginning stages of putting his business plan together and buying his first house. Dana put together a diet program and called it the six-week burn; it went along with working out with him at the gym three times a week. The diet and exercise regime was very successful, and his clients would drop quite a bit of weight in those six weeks and see great results, getting into shape as well as trimmer.

Dana decided he wanted to have his own clothing line, and he hired a person to develop his Bullenbeiser logo: the head of a boxer dog in a diamond shape with the word Bullenbeiser within the diamond and a small star on three of the angles. There were two different versions: one was just the dog and the other was the dog with a pair of boxing gloves dangling from his mouth. It was a great logo, although I have to say I am partial to boxers. They had come up with a different logo before this one: Dana's Doggs in block letters and it looked like a ripped body builder from the waist up and the head was that of a boxer dog on the body. It was actually freaky looking. That logo was nixed for good reason.

We had an attorney conduct a search at the offices of the U.S. Patent and Trademark office in Arlington, Virginia to be sure no one else had the trademark or name Bullenbeiser and Bullenbeiser Boxing Gear or any similar design. On August 21, 1996, we received a letter from the attorney stating their search turned up no pending, current, or abandoned trademark and we were now free to move forward with the trademark.

Strangely, shortly after we filed to register Dana's trademark, he received a letter from a person who claimed to be an attorney for Converse sneakers. The attorney stated that Dana was using a trademark that belonged to Converse and Dana was to cease and desist from using this logo any longer or Converse would take legal action against him. I had already returned to Boston when he received the letter, which Dana faxed to me along with a note: "Mom, I can't afford a lawyer to handle this. What am I supposed to do now?" The logo that this attorney was claiming Dana was stealing from Converse was the star in the three angles of the diamond. I could not believe that anyone would claim to hold the trademark of a symbol of a star. I put a letter together trying to sound very knowledgeable and professional about the whole situation and sent it to the attorney at Converse, asking how they believed they were the only ones who have the right to the use of a star. "What about the American flag, just for starters?" I asked. I told them, by all means, take us to court. I could not wait to see what a judge would have to say about their claim of owning the symbol of a star. We never heard back from them.

Dana decided he wanted to put together a clothing line with t-shirts, hats, sweatshirts, and jackets; but he had no money to get it started. Obviously, the question of money, whether the issue is as small as selling t-shirts or as big as getting the UFC off the ground, is always the point where people either find a way to move forward with their plans and dreams or are forced to give up and walk away. Dana had reached this point.

As I mentioned earlier, I had been out of work waiting for surgery. Fighting with the insurance company over the surgery spread out over a couple of years. It was a nightmare. I had applied for social security disability, and was denied twice before it was finally approved on appeal. I received a check for all the back payments. More than two years worth, this came to around $55,000.00. Unfortunately, I am a spender, as is Dana, and so I would have never saved that kind of money in a million years. Once again, this windfall was a nice twist of fate for Dana.

As a surprise for Dana, I purchased t-shirts, found a silkscreen printer in Cambridge, Massachusetts, and had the logo put on the t-shirts. I chose six different colored shirts and the logo looked great on all of them. I had hundreds of them made up and then shipped them out to Dana in Las Vegas. He loved them. Eventually, I had shorts, sweatpants, sweatshirts, baseball caps, and even leather coats made up with the logo. They looked great and everyone wore them. Dana seemed to be well on his way with his new enterprise in Las Vegas.

The week before Dana's wedding, he stayed at his sister's house. She had bought a four-bedroom, three-bath house on the west side of town. When I flew out for Dana's wedding, I stayed there as well, as did one of my brothers and a friend of Dana's from Boston who was in his wedding. The wedding was over a three-day weekend, and many friends and family had flown in from the east coast for the wedding. Because it was a three-day weekend in Vegas, everyone was in party mode, and at night everyone would head out to meet up with other people in town for the wedding. We would straggle back to Kelly's house at all hours. The house had two floors, and I was in the only bedroom on the first floor. Dana was sleeping in the living room.

A friend of Kelly's had been on a trip a few months before, and she brought a gift back for her: one of those wooden carved dolls and this one was squatting and was wearing just a grass skirt. The figure looked like some voodoo doll from Africa and was quite intimidating and creepy looking. There was a show on television about twenty years ago called *A Trilogy of Terror*, and it really was terrifying. There were three short terrifying tales, and one was about this voodoo doll that this woman gets as a gift; it looked just like the one Kelly had in her house. Of course, the thing comes to life and terrorizes the woman in this story, and after having your stomach in a knot for forty-five minutes, the voodoo doll finally wins.

When I first went into my bedroom, I found this voodoo doll perched on the dresser and the first thing I thought about was that movie. I knew there was no way in hell I was going to be able to sleep as long as that thing was in my room, and so, before I went out for the night, I put it in the living room. When Dana came back to the house that night, he found the voodoo doll in the living room and thought the same thing: no way in hell was he going to have that thing in the room where he was sleeping. He put it back in my bedroom. When I came home rather late that night, or rather, early the next morning, Dana was asleep. I went into my room and the first thing I saw was this voodoo doll back in the bedroom, right where it had been before I removed it. Nothing like having a few cocktails and turning on a light in your bedroom to discover this thing looking at you. I again took it from the bedroom and placed it back in the living room. This time I put it right next to where Dana was sleeping, figuring as he opened his eyes first thing in the morning this would be what would greet him. I thought this will start his day off on a good note.

When I woke up that morning, I went to the kitchen. Dana was sitting in the family room right off the kitchen, and he was looking at me with this shit-eating grin. I could not figure out what was so funny, and so I finally asked him what's going on. He said, "Did you notice anything in your room?"

I asked him what he was talking about, and he went into this full-blown laugh. Then he said, "I put the voodoo doll back in your room last night, and you slept in there with it."

I could not believe he did not see the doll when he woke up because I had put it right in front of his face. I looked at him, grinned, and told him I had moved it back into the living room right next to where he was sleeping. Dana was no longer laughing; he jumped up and ran into the living room to see if the voodoo doll was there. I swear, for the next two days that thing was getting moved all over the house. No one wanted it in the room they were sleeping in. Dana told me that *A Trilogy of Terror* freaked him out and he wished he had never seen it. This doll was freaking every-one out at the house.

As Dana became busier at the gym in the Fertitta building, he would get requests from professional boxers to train in his gym for upcoming fights in Las Vegas. One night Dana ran into John Lewis, a mixed martial arts fighter. Dana was a huge boxing fan but was intrigued by MMA and what was going on in the sport and with the fighters. John agreed to teach Dana Brazilian jiu-jitsu.

Dana felt the fighters in the UFC weren't being represented well and were being paid nothing for their fights. Chuck Liddell, for example was making a $1,000.00 a fight. Dana began manag-ing both Tito Ortiz and Chuck Liddell. Dana and Tito became fast friends, and Dana's relationship with these people would send Dana to Lorenzo with a request that Lorenzo put up the money to buy the UFC, which was failing miserably, indeed about to go under. Dana saw the potential for the sport with the right own-ers and a few changes to the game. Lorenzo listened and thought Dana had something that would be fun and could become a mon-eymaking business, and so the Fertitta's purchased the UFC for two million dollars and thus began the rebirth of the UFC, MMA, and Dana White.

During the first three years that Dana ran the UFC, the Fertittas put forty-four million dollars into the venture. During those early years, my heart went out to Dana. He would call me three or four nights a week, and usually at two or three o'clock in the morning because of the time difference, and talk for an hour about what was going on with the fighters and the UFC, especially all the problems he kept running into. Dana was starting at sub-basement level with the UFC. I would listen to it all. Sometimes a person just needs to unload all their problems at the end of a brutal day. I gave him my opinion on certain things, not that he always listened to what I had to say.

Dana had plenty of brutal days those first couple of years with the UFC. No one wanted anything to do with the UFC at the time. All the athletic commissions refused to sanction the UFC, and the UFC was banned from pay-per-view by most of the cable companies. Dana put rules in place that the athletic commissions were willing to accept, and he started with New Jersey and then moved on to his own state of Nevada. Dana was working around the clock, literally, and the stress was nearly overwhelming. One of his biggest problems was trying to do everything himself. Dana just could not give up control of any little part of the business to anyone, even though he had good people working for him. He just needed to trust that they could do their jobs. I told him in one of our conversations that he just could not keep on like he was, and if he was going to continue with this business, he had to let other people who worked for him start taking over some aspects of the business. Unfortunately, control freaks hate to hand over tasks to others, and even today Dana oversees everything that goes on in UFC.

Dana was spending the Fertitta's money like it was Monopoly money, and he just could not get the UFC over the hump so they could see some return on their investment. I remember the night Dana called to tell me that Lorenzo had said they could not keep losing money and he was pulling the plug. My heart broke for him after all that work and effort he had put into the business, and all the time thinking he was so close to making it work. Fortunately for Dana and the Fertittas, the only person interested in the UFC was willing to pay a meager four million dollars for it. Lorenzo decided to put a little more time and money into the UFC and hope for the best, actually to hope for a miracle.

The Fertittas put ten million dollars into producing *The Ultimate Fighter*, which Spike TV picked up and it became a huge success immediately. The first season finale of *The Ultimate Fighter* was between two light-heavyweights, Stephan Bonner and Forrest Griffin, and the winner would receive a six-figure contract with the UFC. The fight was a toe-to-toe slugfest, and what a fight it was. Dana was so impressed with the way the two fighters finished his first show that he gave them both a contract. Dana and his fighters became an overnight sensation after that, but he still had an uphill battle to bring the UFC to other states and countries and to have MMA accepted as a legitimate up and coming sport.

In 2001, when Dana and the Fertittas first purchased the UFC, they produced a book called the *All New UFC*, and Carmen Electra was their official spokesperson. The book featured six of their fighters: Tito Ortiz, Randy Couture, Jens Pulver, Carlos Newton, Pedro Rizzo, and Chuck Liddell. The purpose of this publication was to launch a marketing campaign to let people know the UFC was under new management and positioning itself to be accepted into the mainstream of MMA and indeed into the mainstream sports world. When Senator John McCain was on his campaign to bring down the UFC, I told Dana how upset I was with all the bad press, especially from McCain. Dana said, "Mom, don't get so worked up over it. For us now, any press is free advertising and helping make people aware of who we are." I was still pissed off by it.

In *USA Today* on April 11, 2005 was an article about Dana and the TUF show: "Despite an 11:05 p.m. ET/PT Monday slot on Spike TV, the average audience grew 19% to 1.98 million through the first 12 weeks of the 13 week show, according to Nielsen Media Research. The elusive, advertiser-coveted audience of men ages 18 to 34 is up 55% since the January opening. Viewers are 73% male, with an average age of 30. Advertisers include Miller, Nintendo and the U.S. Army."

On page two of the *Boston Sunday Globe* on April 26, 2006 in "Personality Parade," which is an opportunity for people to send in questions about movie stars and sports icons, a reader asked, "What is your opinion of the Ultimate Fighting Championship bouts that are becoming the favorite blood sport in Las Vegas and on TV?" The answer to the question was, "We agree with Sen. John McCain, who called that type of sport 'a human cockfight.' It should be banned." After five years of attempting to change people's perception, Dana, the UFC, and the fighters are still viewed by many as part of a brutal, uncivilized sport.

When the UFC began selling DVDs of their fights, the UFC was still struggling. Dana called and asked me to do him a favor. He asked me to make the rounds of the different stores that sell DVDs in Boston and note whether they were carrying the UFC's fight DVDs. If the stores carried them, he wanted me to make sure they were somewhere in the front of the store where everyone would see them. The next day I went to six stores in Boston, my first stop at the Copley Place Mall. Initially, I could not find the DVD, but after about five minutes of searching, I found one UFC DVD in the sports section buried behind about ten other sports DVDs. I took the DVD to the front of the store where they had a rack with new releases, and acted like I was interested in buying something in the rack, I placed the UFC DVD in the front where it could be seen. Of the six stores I went to, only one did not have the DVD, and at every store I found it in, I moved them to the new release rack at the front of the store.

Dana called that night, and I told him that only one out of the six stores did not have the DVD. He said he would look into that store, and he asked me to check the same stores the next day to see if the DVD was still there or if it was sold. The next day at the first store, the DVD was not where I had put it; but just to make sure it had sold, I checked the sports section where I had found it the day before. I found it there, and once again, I moved the DVD to the new release rack in the front of the store. I did the same thing in all the other stores.

Dana again asked if the DVDs were still there. I told him they were and what I had done. Dana asked that I repeat what I had done in a few days, and he asked me to go to a few new stores as well. A few days later, I did as he asked. The next time we spoke, Dana asked me to go to all these stores and add a couple more stores to my route. I told him that, if I kept walking into these stores every day and not buying anything, someone was going to get suspicious and think I was trying to steal something. Moreover, it was taking me all day to run around Boston to all these stores. Dana asked me to please do it one more day and that would be the end of it, and I did. Talk about micromanaging a business. However, today UFC DVDs are the biggest sellers in stores like Wal-Mart, and their video games sell out as soon as they go on the market.

The first fight after Dana purchased the UFC was on February 23, 2001 in Atlantic City, UFC 30 at the Trump Taj Mahal, a 4,500 seat venue. These days, the UFC easily sells out 44,000 seat arenas. I attended every fight for the first three years after Dana purchased the UFC, and in the very beginning, I was often the only family member at the fight. Dana always called a couple days before the fight and asked if I was going to be there. I remember thinking that I was going to the fights to support him and I would just chat with people in attendance because I really wasn't interested in the fights and knew very little about MMA. I was quite amazed when, I found myself jumping to my feet and screaming, "Finish him as one fighter put the other in a chokehold or had just landed a punishing blow to the head and you knew it was all over. I had no idea where that came from, some primal piece of DNA leftover from our ancestral caveman family perhaps.

Maybe a more fitting comparison would be the Romans at the Coliseum. I still find the music and the gladiator at the beginning of UFC pay-per-views so fitting. Eventually, I knew who most of the fighters were and had my favorites, like Chuck Liddell, Randy Couture, Jens Pulver, and Yves Edwards, I would want to see win. I also liked it when Tito Ortiz entered the arena with the American flag, very patriotic. I learned many of the moves and countermoves of the fighters, and knowing these things makes the fights a lot more interesting.

I remember going to UFC 37, High Impact, in Bossier City, Louisiana; and as I was flying over Louisiana and the plane was coming down for the landing, all I could see for miles and miles were trees. I could not even see houses in between the trees. I remember looking out a window, standing in a hallway at the arena, and thinking, "Where are all the people going to come from for this fight? There are no homes. There are no people around here." They did come though — 7,200 was the attendance — and although the UFC did not sell out the arena as they do now, overall; I thought they did pretty well. I believe someone was fired for that one.

UFC 30, 31, and 32 were all in New Jersey. Tank Abbott had come into the building at one of the fights, and as he was walking down the steps to a seat near the ring, the crowd began to chant "Tank, Tank, Tank" over and over and over, they were getting louder and louder with every chant. The UFC had hired Carmen Electra to a six-month contract to be the spokesperson for the UFC. When the crowd started chanting, Lorenzo grabbed Carmen by the hand and brought her to where the cameras could hone in on her and not Tank. They didn't want the crowd caught up in Tank coming in. Dana had told me that, when he and Lorenzo first met with Carmen, they were both surprised by how beautiful she was in person. They thought that she probably looked good on television because of makeup, but that in person she would not be such a beauty. Hiring her actually helped the UFC with publicity that they would not have gotten otherwise.

UFC 33, Victory in Vegas, was at Mandalay Bay and their first fight in Las Vegas. It was on September 28, 2001. Think back two weeks and three days before that date, it was 9/11, when the Twin Towers in New York City were attacked, and the country was still very much in a state of shock. People were terrified that the Twin Towers were only the beginning. People were not flying or traveling, and Dana was sure that people were not going to travel to Las Vegas for his fight with the horror of 9/11 so fresh in everyone's minds. Dana was worried sick that his first Las Vegas show would be a complete failure, and there were quite a few people telling him exactly that: the event was going to fail miserably.

The attendance was 9,500 and the gate was $816,660.00, which was good. This was also the first UFC event sanctioned by the

Nevada State Athletic Commission. The fight was somewhat of a disaster, because most of the fights that night went to a decision, the broadcast ran over and cut out early on the cable stations, leaving all the pay-per-view fans unhappy. They did not get to see the end of the Ortiz-Matyushenko fight. Dana was furious and made changes before the next fight to ensure that would never happened again.

Dana was Tito's manager before he and his partners bought the UFC, and after that first fight in Vegas, Tito became the fighter that Dana and the UFC promoted over all others. The old saying about having all your eggs in one basket were proved true, however. Tito was a great fighter back then, and he came across as a bad boy with some of his antics in the ring, Dana liked that. Dana felt that the fans wanted fighters that came across as badasses. He thought the fans wouldn't go for someone like Randy Couture because he was just too nice and squeaky clean, but Randy was one of my favorite fighters from the beginning and, much to Dana's surprise, the favorite of many, many UFC fans. Tito was UFC's first and biggest superstar, but eventually Tito and Dana would have a falling out. In fact, they truly hated each other for quite a while. Recently they patched things up and Dana brought Tito back to the UFC, but their relation is strained at best. Chuck Liddell started out being managed by Dana also, and Dana and Chuck are still very good friends today.

A year after UFC 33, at UFC 40 at the MGM, the attendance was 13,500 and the gate was $1,540,000.00. At UFC 100 on July 11, 2009, again at Mandalay Bay, attendance was 10,871 and the gate was $5,128,490.00. MMA and the UFC had taken off. The revenue from pay-per-view last year alone was $225,000,000, then add in the sales of all their clothes, DVD's, games, etc. and you come up with a staggering figure. In eight short years, Dana had brought the UFC from a bankrupt business to a multibillion dollar, international empire. Dana had worked nearly around the clock at times, and I still do not know how he keeps his head sufficiently clear to be able to conduct business with so little sleep and so much international traveling, but he does.

Everyone who interviews Dana always asks him how he brought the UFC from nearly bankrupt to the multi-billion dollar international business it is today. First and foremost, he had two billionaire brothers for partners whose deep pockets and all their resources were available to him. They did not restrict Dana in any way in spending their money, and they are obviously very intelligent businessmen, not only running but expanding their other businesses. Dana had developed a passion for the sport himself, and when he talked to people about MMA, you could feel his passion. Dana has a particular personality, and both men and women are drawn to him and want to be his friend. People like being around him and want to help him. For eight years Dana put every waking minute of his life into building the UFC, and he continues to do so because he still sees so much potential for the sport and the business. It was just the perfect time for something new and exciting to come along in the world of sports. Their target audience is eighteen to thirty-four year-old males. In fact, it was kind of like the perfect storm coming together, it was the right time for something new in sports, and Dana and his partners were the right people to pull it all together.

Business schools teach how to build a business by researching and planning your venture, with market analysis and market strategies, a marketing plan, pricing strategies, and strategies for managing and growing a business. Dana had no college, (although he says he does), but he had the ability to recognize an opportunity, to see the global possibilities, and to be able to grow the business with his passion and common sense and not to listen to all the people telling him the business was destined to fail. What Dana has working in his favor cannot be taught in any school: a belief from day one that MMA could replace boxing and become an international sport that is followed by millions of fans all over the world. Then he simply worked around the clock and micromanaged every aspect of the business to bring it to where it is today. However, Dana and the Fertittas also knew from day one that they needed to change the image of the UFC and immediately began a marketing campaign to do that. They have been very smart with the individuals they bring on board to work for them knowing that image, marketing, and the right alliances are everything. They have not missed a step in executing this plan.

Others have tried to compete with the UFC, to ride the coattails of the UFC's success, but none have been successful. Bellator and StrickForce are out there now competing against the UFC, unlike others that tried and failed. The IFL, "the company lost 20 million dollars in 2007 alone." Elite XC, "bad business decisions that ended up turning huge viewership numbers into $55 million in losses." Affliction, "those fights came at a cost, the chance of long term success was nil." Johnathan Snowden, editorial, Bloody Elbow, 2010. It took fifty million dollars to get the UFC over the hump, but besides the money there has to be a commitment of time, lots of someone's personal time. From day one, the UFC's fights have always had a very polished, professional look, and I have yet to see any of the other companies be able to pull that off. The UFC has a president who is driven, passionate about the sport, and ruthless in his dealings, a man who refuses to listen to anyone speaking negatively about the sport, and the way he runs the company.

Just Mauied

WHO IS DANA WHITE TODAY?

Dana and the Fighters.

When Zuffa purchased the UFC, Dana was managing Chuck Liddell, (the Iceman) and Tito Ortiz, (the Huntington Beach Bad Boy) and working very hard to get them better pay for their fights. In those early days, Dana became good friends with many of the fighters, and Tito Ortiz and Dana were very good friends from the moment they first met. They remained friends as long as Dana was only looking out for Tito's best interests, as he should have been.

Back when Tito held the belt in his weight division, Dana came to Boston on business and Tito came with him. Dana always liked to travel with other people rather than by himself, his entourage of one or ten it didn't matter as long as he was not by himself. It was a Sunday morning, and Dana called to say he was coming by to pick me up to go to breakfast. I was living on the first floor of the three-decker in South Boston at the time, and some new people had recently moved in on the second floor, three young guys probably in their early twenties. They had a stereo system that they would crank up full blast, and it was so loud I could not even hear my television when it was on. I had asked them once if they could just keep it down a little because it was really loud in my apartment. They said they would but that didn't happen.

The morning that Dana and Tito came over, the boys upstairs had the music blasting. Dana walked into my apartment, and the first words out of his mouth were, "Are you fucking kidding me?

What the hell is that bullshit?" I told him I had already asked them once not to crank up the music that loud but obviously they didn't care.

Tito said, "I'll take care of this," and he headed up to the second floor. Within a couple minutes, the music had stopped and Tito was back in my apartment. Tito said, "It's been taken care of you shouldn't have any more problems with them." Dana asked Tito what he had done. Tito answered, "I was knocking on their door and they couldn't even hear me. The door was unlocked, so I walked in, and when they saw me, they turned the music down and wanted to know what I was doing in their apartment. I told them my mother-in-law lived downstairs and it would be very much appreciated if they were a little more respectful and kept the music down."

They never did turn the music up loud again, and a few weeks later I ran into one of the boys in the hallway and he asked me if that was Tito Ortiz that had come into their apartment. I told him it was. He said one of the boys recognized him and they had been telling all their friends that Tito was in their apartment and his mother-in-law lived downstairs. They were quite excited about Tito being in their apartment and I am sure they still talk about it today.

The problem with Dana starting out as the fighters' friend and manager is typical with any business. You could compare Dana to a union fighting for better pay and working conditions for the fighters. Once he became part owner and a corporate executive of UFC, however, his goals and priorities were no longer for the employees/fighters but how he could propel the company to be number one in MMA and make as much money as he could for the company. That does not translate into a positive for the fighters. When you start out fighting against management and then you become management, it is very difficult to change hats and still be friends with employees/fighters because their best interests are no longer your best interests. Not that all the fighters still aren't much better off today than they ever were before Dana and the Fertittas took over the UFC, but the transition can have its problems.

The complaint that many of the fighters have is that UFC *is* the fighters, not Dana White. In the *Rolling Stone* article of June 12, 2008, the writer recalls speaking with one of the fighters: "In a private moment, he frowns and says, 'So how come you're doing a story on Dana? I don't understand that. The fighters are what make the sport.'" The fighter is right to a degree. Obviously, there is no UFC without the fighters, but Dana has built the sport to what it is today and he did it by putting his face out there. People associate Dana White with the UFC and in fact tend to think of them as one in the same. The situation is comparable to when Dana started Dana White Enterprises and the Bullenbeiser logo was the symbol of his business. Dana's face is the symbol of the UFC and MMA right now. There are always new fighters coming up, wanting to make a name for themselves and be part of the UFC, but fighters come and go. A fighter's life span in the UFC can be very short lived. Any fighter with a string of loses or who does not put on a good show for the fans, win or lose, find them quickly cut from the UFC.

The fighters may come and go but Dana is always there and a large presence in the UFC and the arena of MMA. From the time Dana was very young, he loved attention. Now he has plenty of attention, and I do not ever see him stepping into the background and letting someone else become the face of MMA and UFC.

Some sports commentators have suggested that maybe the UFC has reached a level where someone who is not so rash, brazen, and arrogant might be a better fit now for Dana's job. Some have publicly stated that someone with a little more polish and education might be the right person for the job now. You can only imagine Dana's response to comments like that.

It is true that Dana has had issues and disagreements with some of the fighters because, with Dana, it is his way or you're out. If you happen to see things in a different light than Dana, you change your way of thinking to his way or you are gone. His motto is: I always do what I want and I always get what I want. I would say that 99.9% of the time this is completely true and creates quite an arrogant person. What kind of person always gets what they want and much of the time takes without asking?

It does not take a whole lot for Dana to get mad at someone and turn on that person with a vengeance, and when he is the one who signs the paycheck, that is not a good thing for that person. Some of those disagreements with fighters have been highly publicized. Some of the fighters thought that, once the public and the fans knew what was going on with their dispute with Dana and the fans got involved in the issue, they would turn on Dana — but once again that has not happened. Those fighters then find themselves on the outside and all they want to do is get back into the UFC and fight again. They quickly realize that going up against Dana is futile.

For example, in 2007 Randy Couture announced he was leaving the UFC and his position as an on-air analyst. Eventually Zuffa filed a lawsuit against Randy and won. Randy is back fighting in the UFC. Tito Ortiz after a number of issues with Dana decided not to re-sign with the UFC and go elsewhere. Tito soon found that move did not work out for him. When Dana asked Tito to forget their past disagreements and return to fight for the UFC, Tito signed a contract to return to the UFC. The newly forged relationship between Dana and Tito has not turned out well for Tito. Matt Linland was another fighter who found himself on Dana's shit list. Matt went to another organization to fight after Dana fired him for wearing an unapproved t-shirt at UFC 54 weigh-ins. Rampage Jackson and Dana had words flying in the press when Rampage wanted a movie career over fighting in the UFC and left the UFC to do a movie, *The A Team*. Rampage is now back fighting in UFC. Both Ken and Frank Shamrock have had words in the press with Dana and there was a lawsuit with Ken Shamrock. Pat Miletich went to the IFL and paid for that with Dana, there is no love lost there. Greg Jackson, a well-known and admired MMA trainer who runs a training camp in Albuquerque, New Mexico has been on the negative side of Dana in the press lately. Those are just a few of the fighters who, unfortunately for them, went up against Dana. In almost every case, the result was not very favorable for them.

Dana remains King of MMA and does not intend to give up his throne or his kingdom. He is the king who rules with an iron fist and everyone is expected to do his bidding or face the executioner. If anything, he continues to conquer other countries with the expansion of the UFC. Dana claims that the UFC fights are seen in 500 million homes on some form of television, and he says, with a few deals they have in the works, that number will soon be one billion. In 2009, the UFC hired an individual to head their Asian Operations division, which covers China, Japan, Korea, Taiwan, Hong Kong, and Southeast Asia. You will find Dana on the cover of Kampiro Magazine, (December 2010) with a newly signed Japanese fighter. China alone has a population of 1.3 billion people, a majority of whom are in the UFC's primary demographic target. Obviously, Dana wants nothing less than global dominance not only in the world of MMA but the sports world.

CHANGES

Obviously, the UFC took off as Dana had envisioned and only continues to grow every year, but along the way, Dana changed. I suppose it was inevitable, but his friends and family just were not prepared for the ways in which he would change and how much of a change it would be, especially to those closest to him. As his career and the UFC took off, the goodness of his character seemed to plummet.

Have you ever heard Dana mention his family, ever, in interviews, on radio, television or just in conversation? I don't mean his wife or children, but his grandmother, mother, sister, niece, nephew, uncles, aunt. He never mentions any of them, and there is a reason, a reason I find to be an embarrassment for all of us but especially an embarrassment to me, as his mom.

After the first four years when the UFC turned around and started making a profit, we began to notice changes in Dana. In the beginning we chalked the changes up to the stress Dana was under and just dismissed it. In hindsight, that was probably not the best way to handle these changes. Later, I realized Dana's changes were more than just the products of stress. He was becoming a total prick to everyone, and by everyone I mean his family and friends who were there for him whenever he needed them, before Dana and the UFC were a success. To UFC fans, Dana is the King of MMA, but I cannot express how overwhelmingly disappointed I am in him as a son, grandson, brother, and uncle. He shows little respect for women, from the way he treats his own mom, grand-mother, girlfriends, wife, sister, niece, and employees, to his very public rant at a female reporter.

Dana's family attended many of the fights in the early years when Frank and Lorenzo Fertitta had first purchased the UFC. We all paid for airfare from the east coast and for our hotel rooms once in in Las Vegas. This was expensive for those of us who attended the fights frequently but everyone wanted to be there to support Dana, (at least we did not have to pay for the tickets to the fights) and we had great seats. We all had a good time when we would attend the fights. One weekend we were in Las Vegas for a fight at Mandalay Bay and Randy Couture was one of the main event fights. Myself, Dana, two of my brothers, and a few other people were walking down the hallway to Dana's suite and I was speaking with someone about Randy, (and by the way, I adore Randy, he is so Captain America). Dana was walking about ten feet in front of me when he yells, "Why don't you shut the fuck up? You don't know anything." I knew he spoke that way to his fight-ers and employees, but I never expected he would talk to me like that. I'm his mom, who says that to their mom? I didn't respond, I didn't know how to respond to what had just happened. Later, when Dana was no longer with us, everyone said, "don't let what Dana just said bother you, he's under a lot of stress and he didn't mean it." I thought the same thing and just let it go, although an apology at any point would have gone a long way.

At every fight, Dana always asked me if I was going to the press conference. In the beginning, everyone wanted to go to the press conferences, but soon it was only me going. Everyone else wanted to get to the after-fight parties. I'm sure people would find it hard to believe, but many of the men who make their living fighting in the octagon are extremely religious. On occasion, you'll hear one of them say in an after-fight interview that they thank God or Jesus for their success, (a lot also thank their moms). In these press con-ferences I attended, when the winners of the fights spoke, many started out by thanking God, and saying that, without His help, they would not have the success they have. At one of the press conferences in 2004, a Brazilian fighter who fought Randy for the light heavyweight championship was in tears as he spoke because his sister had been kidnapped a month before (and it would be years later before four people were arrested for her kidnapping and murder). He said it was only with the help of Jesus that he was able to get up every day and move forward. I had a lump in my throat listening to him, and I think everyone else in the room did. There is a little irony in all of this because Dana claims to be an atheist.

After the press conference was finished I would wait while Dana talked privately with the MMA press and fighters, and then we would head out for the after-fight party. It would take us anywhere from thirty minutes to an hour to get through the casino and hotel lobby because of all the fans still around in the hotel after the fights. The minute they saw Dana walking by, they would stop him to ask him for a picture or autograph or just to talk with him and let him know how much they loved the fights and what he had done with the UFC and the sport of MMA. One positive thing I can say about Dana: he is very aware that the fans are the ones who have made the UFC the success it is. He always has time for the fans and is always nice and polite to them, and in fact, I never once heard him complain about the fans or try to avoid them.

At an after-fight party one night we were in a suite at Mandalay Bay around 4 a.m., and there were maybe twenty of us still sitting around talking. I walked over and sat on a sofa near Dana, he was sitting in a chair next to the sofa talking with eight or ten people who worked for Zuffa, some of the executives and their wives. I started to join in the conversation, and had barely gotten a full sentence out when Dana cut me off. He said, "Shut the fuck up. Nobody wants to hear anything you have to say."

At first, there was an extremely uncomfortable silence after his response to my entering into the conversation, and everyone was just looking at each other. I didn't know most of the people sitting there, and I wasn't sure if they even knew I was Dana's mom. Dana rarely introduced me to people. I'm not sure what that was all about, but at this particular moment I didn't know what to think about his disrespectful comments to me, nor did anyone else. I thought for a brief second that maybe Dana thought it was funny and he was just joking and it came out wrong, but after a few seconds, I realized that wasn't the case. The situation was extremely awkward, and it seemed like the silence was lasting forever, so I began to speak again. Without looking at me, Dana said, "Shut the fuck up." Then turned his back toward me and started a conversation with the group sitting there. I could not believe he had just done that and it took everything in me not to have a knee jerk response to the situation, but I graciously and with great restraint took the high road and didn't do or say anything in front of everyone. His disrespectful behavior catapulted him into the total inconsiderate prick category.

I have no idea where Dana got his filthy mouth because when he was growing up I didn't swear in front of Dana or his sister. At times, I don't know how he can possibly make a comprehensible sentence with the f-bombs used as every other word.

After everyone left the party, I went to bed for a couple hours, but was still so angry I couldn't sleep. After a few hours of lying in bed just steaming and wondering why Dana would behave like that towards me, I just couldn't lay there any longer, I got up, showered and went to Dana's bedroom and woke him and Anne. They were in the second bedroom of the suite. I asked Dana why he spoke to me like that, especially in front of other people. He said, "No one wants to hear some drunk telling a story that they wouldn't be interested in." He had no idea what I was going to say.

I said, "I was not drunk." I was flying back to Boston that day and I don't drink when I fly. I get airsick on planes and I didn't need to add to it by being hung over. The drink I had in my hand at the party was club soda with lime, no booze. Why he assumed I was drunk, I don't know but I told him, "that had better never happen again," and once again, there was no apology. That he found it appropriate to behave in that manner, I don't understand. The fights were over and he was sitting around with friends talking and enjoying himself. We couldn't blame it on stress this time. His behavior was intentionally mean and spiteful, and so began the reign of the King of MMA, Dana the tyrant.

When Dana first began teaching boxing aerobics classes in the gyms and clubs in Las Vegas, one of his students was a young woman who absolutely loved taking his classes and loved Dana. She had lost weight and gotten into terrific shape taking the classes Dana taught. Eventually she started working for Dana in his gym, helping teach classes and working with private clients.

When the Fertittas purchased the UFC, she moved along with Dana as his personal secretary. She did everything for him, from running errands to paying his personal bills to traveling with him to all the fights. When you work for Dana, you are on call for him 24/7. He expects you to put in the same hours he does, and she did, but I can also say she loved it. She traveled with him to all the fights and her husband had started working for UFC as well.

At one of the early fights in New Jersey, I was speaking with her when she confided in me that Dana had not been treating her civilly. She said Dana would berate and belittle her in front of everyone, ranting, screaming, and swearing at her over the slightest issue. A couple of times he had brought her to tears. I was bothered by her comments, and I told her that was out of line for Dana to treat her or any other employee that way. I told her she didn't have to put up with that kind of behavior from him. I said I would speak to him about his behavior, but she asked me not to say anything to him. She didn't want to start something that would create an even worse atmosphere for her at work.

Soon after she had spoke with me she went to Lorenzo, one of Dana's partners, thinking Lorenzo was Dana's boss and that Lorenzo had the final word. She was under the impression that she could talk to him about an issue she was having with Dana. Lorenzo told Dana she had come to him, and Dana hearing this went ballistic and fired her. She was devastated; they had been together for years. She was someone who was with Dana from the earliest days, when he was just starting out teaching exercise classes in the gyms in Las Vegas and had no money.

She eventually went to work for the IFL. Dana was furious when any of his former employees went to work for other MMA organizations that were trying to compete with the UFC. Employees now have to sign a "no compete" clause, so if they leave the UFC they cannot go to work for any competitors of the UFC for a specified amount of time. Dana has a reputation for being ruthless and going after anyone he feels has said or done anything he doesn't like with a vengeance, and so the "no compete" clause tends to work. Anyone who has ever worked for Dana knows Dana is dangerous and vengeful and will take legal action in a heartbeat.

The UFC sued the IFL for illegally using proprietary information obtained by hiring executives from the UFC. The UFC also accused the IFL of trying to buy out top UFC fighters. The IFL filed their own lawsuit against the UFC claiming the UFC was threatening potential partners not to work with the IFL. In July 2008, word began to spread in the MMA community of the UFC's possible purchase of the IFL. That same month, the IFL closed and many of their fighters were now fighting in the UFC.

Dana was becoming a spiteful tyrant. It obviously didn't matter who you were — family, friends, fighters, employees — if you said or did the slightest thing that he didn't like; he was going after his piece of flesh. Going after you with all the considerable resources he has at hand. He would scream and swear at employees and fighters in front of everyone for the slightest issue, publicly belittling them, but worse, Dana would be hell bent to destroy whoever the person was who would dare say or do anything he didn't like. I was at a loss as to where such hostility came from. In that same *Rolling Stone* article dated June 12, 2008, one of the fighters said, "'Most fighters won't say anything critical of White.' Then he stops to think, and what he says next is 'Don't use any of what I just said. Please. I will hunt you down. You don't understand how this guy operates. He will destroy me.' He's probably right about that. Unless you spend some time on White's bad side, you can't get a complete picture of the guy and what he is capable of."

The writer then tells how Matt Linland was fired by Dana, how Dana claimed, "He fucked me, and he knows he fucked me."

This was all over a t-shirt Matt wore. Obviously, it took very little to get on Dana's shit list, and in fact half the time the person never even realized they had done anything to deserve Dana's wrath. Later in that same article, the writer says, "Another person who has felt White's wrath is his mother. White got mad at her three years ago, some big family thing he won't go into, and hasn't spoken to her since." I could not believe Dana would tell a complete stranger something like that and allow it to be printed in an article in *Rolling Stone*. Dana's statement and his disrespect toward his own mom was shameful. Dana told the writer he did not want to talk about the big family thing that he and I were no longer speaking over, and if I were Dana I wouldn't want anyone to know what it was either. Dana insinuated that his family had done something disrespectful to him. Where the hell does that come from? If that were truly the case and somehow we had done something to be hurtful or spiteful I could understand, but that was not the case.

Dana should have felt guilty and sorry for what he did. He should have apologized to his sister and to me; but instead he went around acting as if everyone else had done something wrong. He told people we owed him an apology for disrespecting him. I don't even know where that statement comes from?

Kelly, Dana's sister, is godmother to Dana's son, Aidan; and when her second child, Gillian, was born, she asked Dana to be godfather. Dana said yes, but trying to find time when Dana was free to come back east for the christening was very difficult. Kelly had cancelled and rescheduled the christening twice after Dana told her he had to be somewhere else on business and could not get out of the commitment. That was not true, however. The second time he called Kelly, he told her he had to be in Japan on business when he actually went to the Bahamas with the Fertittas on their yacht. When I found out what he had done, I told him, "I'm not getting in the middle of this. You better not let your sister know you lied to her and the real reason you blew off Gillian's christening." Finally, the third time the christening was scheduled, Dana came back with Anne and the two boys, Dana and Aidan, and decided to stay for a week and visit with friends and family. The christening was to be at the end of their visit.

The day before the christening, we were at the beach house at Hampton Beach and Dana was in a foul mood. He decided he wanted to go back to Boston and go out for the night. Most of us just wanted to hang out at the beach house with the kids. We didn't get to see Dana's children that often, and they were leaving in two days, but even then it was all about Dana. Everyone headed back to Boston, and Dana reserved a room at a club for a party that night. I had stayed at the beach to pick up the house, and Dana called to ask if I was coming to Boston. I told him I was on my way. He then asked me to stop at the Boston Harbor Hotel and pick up Niko, Kelly's son, and bring him to Kelly's house. I said sure. When I got to the Boston Harbor Hotel, I called my sister, who was in the hotel room, and asked her to bring Niko down to me. I was parked in front of the hotel waiting. When she came down, she told me Dana and Aidan, who were four and three respectively at the time, were crying because they wanted to stay with Niko, who was three, and didn't want him to leave. I told my sister to get Dana and Aidan ready and I would take them with me to Kelly's house.

I then called Dana to let him know that the boys were going with me. He began screaming and swearing that they weren't going anywhere, that they were staying in the hotel. I explained they were crying and wanted to be with Niko. Dana said, "I don't give a fuck what they want they'll get over it." I left the boys at the hotel and took Niko home. I stayed at Kelly's house for about half an hour then, I went home to my place in Boston to shower and get dressed in preparation for meeting Dana at the club. Everyone who was going out for the night were all already there with him. I called him three or four times, and every time the call went straight to his voice mail. I tried calling one of my brothers who was with Dana, and his phone went straight to voicemail. I didn't know what club they were at, and so I figured they would check their phones in a little while, see I had called, and call me back to let me know where they were, but no one ever did call me back. I gave up and went to bed, I thought it was just as well that I wouldn't be out half the night before the christening.

The christening was at noon the next day at a church in Quincy, Massachusetts and of course I was running late. I was on my way to the drugstore on the corner near my house to get a card, planning to head over to Kelly's house after that, when my sister called. She asked, "What are you doing?" I said, "I'm running late and I need to get to Kelly's before everyone leaves because I don't know where the church is." My sister replied, "Oh they're still going to have the christening?"

I was confused by her statement and asked, "What are you talking about?"

She proceeds to tell me that Dana was not going to the christening that he had called for his jet and was packing and leaving Boston. I couldn't even grasp what she was saying. I called Dana's cell phone and it went straight to voicemail. I called the hotel and asked for Dana's room, and the receptionist said, "no calls are to be put through to that room." I felt sick to my stomach; I really felt like throwing up. I couldn't begin to think why Dana was going to do this to his sister and his niece, his only sister and only niece. I drove about a hundred miles an hour over to the Boston Harbor Hotel, pulled up out front, left my car running, and ran through the lobby and over to the elevators. When I reached Dana's room, I began pounding on the door. My brother, who had spent the night there, opened the door in a bathrobe. I'm thinking, it's an hour until the christening, and the hotel is twenty-five minutes from the church!

I went flying into the room. Anne was sitting in the living room in her bathrobe with the two boys, eating breakfast and watching television. Dana was in one of the bedrooms packing. I said, "What the hell is going on?" He tells me they are leaving. I asked, "What about the christening?"

Dana replied, "I don't give a fuck about the christening and we aren't going. We are flying home to Las Vegas now." At that point, Dana and I are screaming at each other. He says, since we could not be bothered to go to his party at the club, then he was not going to the christening. He then added that Kelly's husband had called him and really pissed him off, telling Dana that he and Kelly were not going to the party because they were not jumping on the Dana money train like everyone else (to that I'll just say, "My, how things change"). I could NOT believe Dana was really going to do this; it was just inconceivable to me. On the way out of the hotel room, I grabbed his son and said, "You're coming with Grammy." If I had not taken him with me when I left, Dana would have never showed up at the church for Gillian's christening.

Dana and Anne finally did make an appearance five minutes late. Just before they arrived, Kelly kept asking, "Where are Dana and Anne? Someone call them and find out where they are." I didn't tell Kelly what had just gone on at the hotel. I didn't want to ruin the whole day for her. When the christening was over, Dana disappeared before I could talk to him.

Kelly had reserved a room at a restaurant for drinks and dinner after the christening. Everyone headed over to the restaurant. At first I thought Dana had gotten lost or stopped on the way to get something. I thought, if they were lost, he would really be in an ugly mood when he showed up. Finally, my brother tells us, "Oh Dana's gone, he left to go back to Las Vegas. His jet was waiting for him." My brother proceeds to tell Kelly that Dana was not even going to go to the christening but I had taken little Dana from the hotel and he had to come and get him. Of course upon hearing this his sister is devastated. She could not understand why Dana would have done this to her. Through the whole dinner, all she did was cry. An event that should have been so happy and special, Dana made sure he ruined for everyone. I had had it with him after his complete disrespect for his sister and the christening. That was the big family thing that Dana didn't want to talk about with the writer from *Rolling Stone*, the reason Dana and I didn't speak for a long time.

In that same article in *Rolling Stone* is a section titled "The Wisdom of Dana White," and one subtitle is "Women." Dana stated to the writer, "What I've learned from women is they're all fucking crazy. You find one that deals with your craziness and make the best. The grass is never greener." If anyone knows from whence he speaks, it is Dana. There has been plenty, and I do mean plenty, of grass that he thought was greener. He makes Tiger look like a choirboy. I have news for my son: not all women are crazy. Between your wife and your sister-in-law (he calls her his second wife, and I won't even go down that road), you've just become so used to women who are mean and nasty in your life that you think it's normal.

Dana and his wife honeymooned in Hawaii after their wedding. When they returned to Las Vegas from the honeymoon, Dana had one of the worst black eyes I've ever seen. It was horrifying. When he first came home from his honeymoon, he told everyone he had jumped on the bed at the hotel, overshot the bed, and hit the bedside table. I knew that wasn't true, I can tell when he's lying, and later he told me what had really happened. He said his new wife blindsided him with a vase or a lamp, knocking him unconscious and splitting his eye open. The hotel staff called an ambulance to take him to the emergency room, where he received stitches to close the gash just above his eye. If the cut had been any lower, he would have lost his eye. This type of behavior goes on constantly. They are always fighting, and she is the physical abuser. Money sometimes does not fix everything, but then, some things just cannot be fixed.

I was with one of Dana's friends in Las Vegas one day, and he said to me, "I wish I could find someone like Dana has for a wife."

I looked at him and I said, "Watch out what you wish for." He was quite surprised by my comment and wanted to know what I meant by it. I said, "I'm not going to say any more." He saw me about a year later and said, "I know what you meant by your statement that day in Las Vegas." He said he had recently spent two weeks with Dana and Anne in Las Vegas.

I can't stand to be in an atmosphere of constant fighting and the stress it creates for everyone. People who create those situations are selfish and inconsiderate, and it was obvious Anne could care less about anyone else. I cannot stand the thought of spending time in a house where everyone is fighting and miserable, that was Dana and Anne's house. How sad, they seem to have everything, (that money can buy) and they are two miserable people.

Dana likes to gamble, and that was true even before all the success and money. There was an assortment of weekend sports betting and playing the roulette tables. He would play the same numbers all the time on the roulette tables, which actually worked out for him because he seemed to win quite often. When Dana bought his first house up in northwest Las Vegas, on Sunday mornings when I was visiting, Dana and I would shoot down to one of the casinos near his house and place all kinds of bets on the football games. I especially liked to bet the over/under bets. I thought they were no brainers, and then we would head home with our stack of tickets. For the rest of the day, Dana and I were glued to the television. I never found football very exciting until I bet on the games. Dana and I would be changing stations trying to follow a half dozen games and hollering and screaming at all the players that were screwing up our bets. In a recent article, the reporter following Dana around said they stopped off to gamble for a few minutes before a weigh-in, and in no time at all Dana lost half a million dollars and just shrugged it off as no big deal. It must be nice that he can do that these days and not think twice about it.

It's funny because as he became wealthy it was obvious he was new money. Have you ever heard that expression as to whether someone comes from old money or is new money. I remember a story Dana told me about being at Morton's Steak House in Las Vegas. He had stepped outside for something when a man waiting at valet collapsed and fell to the ground striking his head so hard on the curb he was bleeding. Dana said he ran over to the man to see if he was all right and had knelt down next to him and somehow had touched the man getting blood on his shirt. He proceeds to tell me he was wearing an eight hundred dollar shirt that he ruined because of the bloodstain he got on it. I didn't know anyone made eight hundred dollar shirts and even if they did why would you pay that much for a shirt. It's not like anyone is going to know it was eight hundred dollars unless you tell them.

I'm sure he didn't realize it but he was always telling every-one how much he paid for things. He would say, "Do you know how much that cost." It got old real quick with everyone, especially when you are someone struggling to pay your day to day bills.

As the UFC began to grow, so did Dana's power both in his business dealings and personal relationships. Suddenly everyone had to be careful around him. If Dana didn't like something a person said or did and he became mad at you, then no one was to talk to you or socialize with you. Everyone would shun you because they didn't want Dana to turn on them. Dana would make it quite clear if you remained friends with the ousted individual then you were no longer welcome around him. Nothing like ruling by intimidation. I remember watching an episode of *The Outer Limits* one night a long time ago. The story was about a little boy with some very strange powers. If someone said or did anything the boy didn't like, he would wish them away to the cornfield, which apparently was a horrifying place to be sent to. That is the way it was becoming around Dana and Anne. Dana's employees, friends, family, and fighters all have to be on guard when they're around him. They don't want to say or do anything that might upset him or they could end up in the cornfield.

Dana and I did begin to speak again about a year after the chris-tening incident, but it was very strained. Dana was treating friends and family in a manner that I found unacceptable. When the UFC began to take off, I would always tell Dana, "Keep your feet on the ground. Remember who cared about you and supported you, who your friends were before all this took off."

He would always say the same thing every time: "I know. I'm not going to change. Don't worry about that, Mom." But he did change. Dana has stated in interviews that family is the most important thing to him, and yet he has treated his entire family — mother, father, grandmother, sister, aunts, uncles, niece and nephew — with utter disregard. It is easy for Dana to make statements to the press that sound good, but those of us who truly know Dana know they are not true.

When Dana was trying to get his business up and running in Las Vegas, he would always say to me, "Mom, one day I'm going to be rich and you'll never have to work or worry about anything." I never really thought that he would ever be as wealthy as he has become, but it is always a nice thing for a mom to hear from her son. His promise was never to be fulfilled either. His wealth has actually become an embarrassment to me, he is selfish, self absorbed and inconsiderate.

I love the thought of sharing good fortune and helping others out. I don't understand why Dana doesn't share that same attitude. With all the success and good fortune Dana has had, he should be very generous and want to help others. His grandmother who lived with us in Las Vegas, drove him to school and fixed dinner for him is now 93 years old and lives in a trailer in Florida. She lives on her meager monthly retirement check, and has lived in a trailer for the last forty years of her life. Dana has done nothing to be sure that she is comfortable and that she doesn't have to stress over having money for everyday living expenses at her age. She drives an older model car and when she travels to visit children, grand children and great grand children, she pays for her own tickets and flies coach. So much for having a grandson who is a multimillionaire with his own jet. When Dana first began to make his million's he did send her a check for 5 thousand dollars and she cried when she opened the envelope and saw it. That was eight years ago and since then he has never done anything else for her. Dana can lose a million dollars gambling in a few hours and just shrug it off, but he can't help out his 93 year old grandmother.

This January Dana's grandmother became ill and had a massive heart attack. Dana called her, (thinking she had very little time left) and told her he was going to send his private jet to pick her up and bring her to Vegas to stay at his house. He told her she would have the best doctors available and around the clock nurses to take care of her. She told all her neighbors and friends that her grandson was sending for her to take care of her while she was sick. She would be living with him in Vegas until she was better, and she wouldn't have to worry about anything. Finally, I thought

138

he was stepping up to the plate to help her, better late than never. She apparently hung in there too long, at least longer than what Dana thought. Dana never called her back and never did anything to help her. I called him twice but he didn't return my calls. His uncle had lunch with him and asked if he was still going to help his grandmother, he never responded to him. Dana's grandmother died on, Sunday, May 1, 2011 at 1 am without ever hearing another word from her grandson, never receiving a card or flower from him, without him doing anything for her. You cannot begin to imagine how crushing and heartbreaking this has been to me to have this have happened to her in her last weeks on this earth. Imagine your grandson who you helped care for and who is filthy rich, never doing anything to make your last years, last weeks, last days on this earth comfortable.

This is not all about money, but the principle of the whole thing. It is about character, about being a man and a good person. I thought I had raised Dana to be a better person, to be thoughtful and kind to others. He certainly was when he was younger, but I guess it's true that money and power corrupt. I certainly never would have dreamed that my son Dana would become the callous and heartless person he is now, cruel, self-centered, and thoughtless.

Maybe my thoughts of that soulless baby forty-two years ago were not so unfounded. Dana has made it big, very big, and has turned his back on his family and friends who were there for him when he needed help and support through the lean, tough times before he became Mr. UFC, King of MMA. Dana once said to me, "Mom, I have so much money that I will never be able to spend it all in my lifetime, no matter what I buy, nor will my kids be able to spend it all in their lives." He said, "I pay more in taxes than you'll ever make in your lifetime." I guess the thought of my not having to work is foreign to him.

Dana has cut ties with most of his old friends as well as his family. Two years ago, Dana was going to make a movie or a weekly show about the Irish mob in Southie, and many of the locals came to audition for bit parts. Dana told me that the producer did not choose any of his friends from Southie who had auditioned, several of whom have had bit parts in other movies. I said, "You're paying for the show. Can't you tell the producer you want them to get some small part?"

Once again, surprise, surprise, he says, "Why the fuck should I?"

I answered, "Because they're your friends and they'd do it for you."

I was thinking about Dana a few months ago, and I was thinking about parents whose children do something that is horrifying in the eyes of society. The first thing everyone says is, "What was wrong with the parents? Couldn't they see it coming?" Or they say, "What did they do in raising that person that made them turn out the way they did?" That is what I keep asking myself. What did I do, or what didn't I do, that Dana turned into the person he is today? I don't understand. Although thinking about Dana's father who is self-centered and cares only about himself, it makes me think maybe genes matter more than how a person is raised.

Dana's fans love him and think he rocks for what he has done with the UFC and MMA. I'm sure that will not change for him, but I am tired of stories about his life that aren't anywhere near the truth. Dana was very loved and cared for growing up, and he was a sweet, loving, and special little boy. When he got older, Dana was a good friend to many people and a good son for many years. What changed him, I can only wonder. I am just disappointed in my son, my only son, my oldest child, the President of the UFC, the King of MMA.

Made in the USA
Las Vegas, NV
16 December 2022

63130204R00085